Louise Arnold — Invisible
friend

INSIDE BLEAK HOUSE

Wolves —
Sweets
A brush with the past
Shirley Hughes

D0755664

Sketch of Dickens by Leslie Ward ('Spy'), 1870

INSIDE
BLEAK HOUSE

*

John Sutherland

Duckworth

First published in 2005 by
Gerald Duckworth and Co. Ltd
90-93 Cowcross Street
London EC1M 6BF
inquiries@duckworth-publishers.co.uk
www.ducknet.co.uk

A CIP catalogue record for this book is available
from the British Library

ISBN 0 7156 3459 3

Typeset by Ray Davies
Printed in Great Britain by
Bookmarque Ltd, Croydon, Surrey

Contents

List of Plates

Introduction

The Victorian experience

The BBC's adaptation of *Bleak House* advertised itself, some six months ahead of time, as intending to use the format of the 'Soap Opera', in an epic collision of Dickens meets *Eastenders*. It was daring scheduling. Directing a twice-weekly double-bore blast of Dickens at the viewing public ran the risk of – well – doubly boring them. Even with the Great Inimitable there is such a thing as Dickens fatigue (nor, to be honest, has *Eastenders* been looking all that fresh recently – *Bleak House* may well pull in more viewers than the soap's current six million audience figure, although Andrew Davies and Nigel Stafford Clark would be only too happy with that figure).

For the literary historian (not, alas, a major presence among the viewing six million) there was an historical appropriateness in the BBC's decision to broadcast *Bleak House* in sixteen snappy half-hour instalments. Dickens's novel was itself first published as a monthly, illustrated serial in nineteen 32-page instalments (the last a 'double') between March 1852 and September 1853 and priced at one shilling (or 5p in today's money) a part. The difference was that Dickens's instalments carried advertising. The BBC's don't (yet).

The serialist, then and now, works in two dimensions – that of the part and that of the whole. It's a tricky balance. Overstress the one, and the narrative becomes episodic – 'bitty'. Overstress the other, and it becomes slack, like a rubber band which has lost its elasticity. Above all, every instalment has to have its 'hook'. Lose a viewer at any stage and you've probably lost them for good.

Dickens was as much a master of 'make 'em *laugh*, make 'em *cry*, make 'em *wait*, make 'em *come back*' as the writing teams who come up with the never-ending storylines swirling around Albert Square and the 'Street'. Dickens, for example, knew just as well as those who devised the demise of Dirty Den, that one of the ways to bump up reading/viewing figures was to wield the executioner's axe. In his working notes for the fifteenth serial episode of the novel, he queried, apropos his pathetic street waif ('He wos wery good to me, he wos') Jo, to whom every reader's heart had gone out: 'Jo? Yes. Kill him'. The poor unsuspecting urchin was slaughtered by his creator as heartlessly as the turkey Scrooge ordered from another little street urchin for Christmas. Or as heartlessly as the BBC schedulers battered Dirty Den to death after Leslie Grantham had been caught doing even dirtier things than usual in front of his computer screen.

Jo went the way of Little Nell and Paul Dombey. A tear-jerking deathbed scene could always be relied upon to drive up Dickens's sales (Den's demise, similarly, got *Eastenders'* highest viewing figures of 2005 – unfortunately the bastard could only be resurrected once). Shocked Victorian readers in May 1853 wept inconsolably for their loss and, more importantly, signed on to *Bleak House* for the duration. Dickens would get his shillings.

As a fellow serialist, Dickens would have admired the 'curtain lines' (or cliffhangers), the cross-cutting, the finely judged alternations of comedy, sentiment, and pathos we get today in *Eastenders*. As an inveterately cockney novelist – 'Boz' – he would also have felt comfortable with the location (how does *Bleak House* begin? With the one-word sentence: 'London').

Above all Dickens would heartily have approved of the 'soap' association in soap opera. Why are they called soaps? Because, in the 1950s, when they began to dominate afternoon television in the United States, the serials were sponsored by the big detergent firms, aimed at middle-class housewives with nothing to do in the afternoon but watch the box, load the washer (another newfangled gadget) and wait for junior to come home from school, and hubby from work for his evening martini and the news programmes. Hence 'soap opera'.

Sanitary Reform – soap for the nation – at the period he was writing *Bleak House*, was an obsession with Dickens – his *idée fixe*, his hobby-horse, his mania, one of the few topics on which he could be boring. 'In all my writings,' he wrote in his Preface to the 1844 novel, *Martin Chuzzlewit*, 'I hope I have taken every available opportunity of showing the want of sanitary improvements in the neglected dwellings of the poor'. Soap-fiction, in a word, was what interested Dickens the most. One finds the obsession with cleanliness (next to Godliness, as the Victorian proverb put it) everywhere in *Bleak House*.

Dickens's filth-meter is always turned on. It goes into whirring overdrive in such scenes as that of the first visit to the brickmakers' hovel, in St Albans. 'Is my daughter a-washin?' asks the drunken brute of a brickmaker, in response to Mrs Pardiggle's condescending enquiries as to the state of his soul and whether he has read the uplifting tracts she has kindly left him:

> Yes, she *is* a-washin. Look at the water. Smell it! That's wot we drinks. How do you like it, and what do you think of gin, instead? An't my place dirty? Yes, it is dirty – it's nat'rally dirty, and it's nat'rally unwholesome; and we've had five dirty and onwholesom children, as is all dead infants, and so much the

better for them, and for us besides. Have I read the little book wot you left? No, I an't read the little book wot you left.

What does Esther (the incarnation of salvationary soap) leave behind her? Why a freshly laundered handkerchief of course.

A year after *Bleak House*'s publication Florence Nightingale and her band of nurses set out to attack the Augean filth at the military hospital at Scutari. As they neared the Crimea, one of her girls – of a somewhat Pardiggle cast of mind – exclaimed, as their vessel came into port:

> 'Oh, dear Miss Nightingale, when we land, let there be no delays, let us get straight to nursing the poor fellows!' 'The strongest will be wanted at the washtub,' was Miss Nightingale's answer.

The Lady with the Lamp and the man with his pen were of one mind. Go for the dirt, not the soul, if you want to do good in this world. Rub a dub dub.

In a speech to the Metropolitan Sanitary Association (for whom the author of *Bleak House* was an all-conquering hero) ten months before the launch of *Bleak House*, Dickens declared his great mission as a reforming novelist:

> I can honestly declare tonight, that all the use I have … made of my eyes – or nose [*laughter*] that all the information I have since been able to acquire through any of my senses, has strengthened me in the conviction that Searching Sanitary Reform must precede all other social remedies [*cheers*] and that even Education and Religion can do nothing where they are most needed, until the way is paved for their minstrations by Cleanliness and Decency [*hear, hear*]. What avails it to send a Missionary to me, a miserable man or woman living in a foetid Court, where every sense upon me for delight becomes a torment, and every minute of my life is new mire added to the

heap under which I lie degraded? To what natural feeling within is he to address himself? … But give me my first glimpse of Heaven through a little of its light and air – give me water – help me to be clean.

'Help me to be clean': that is what the unfortunates who crowd the pages of *Bleak House* are saying.

Plate 1. Flushing the Sewers of London

'The English', wrote a German historian, 'think that soap is civilization'. By that measure, as by others, Dickens is the great English novelist. Note, for example, how Esther handles the Jellyby household, tearing into its mess and clutter like a white tornado, making all 'tidy' and reducing the house's 'marshy' smell to something more breathable. The name of the child whom she bathes, 'changes', and reads to is 'Peepy' (get it?). It is probably the first clean water the little fellow has felt since his baptism.

The chimneys belch smoke in *Bleak House* (see the first paragraph) but the people, in general (Trooper George excepted), don't. The great tobacco boom would happen five years later, when soldiers from the Crimea brought the vogue for the 'Turkish' cigarette back to England (there is, oddly, a premonitory appearance of the cigarette late in the novel, in a glancing reference to Spanish refugees). Ironically, one of the reasons the English adopted the 'gasper' so wholeheartedly was for its usefulness as a fumigator. While we regard the foul emissions of cigarettes as pollution, the Victorians welcomed them as a satisfactory room freshener, eliminating the lingering 'marshy' smell that haunted interiors at the time. About the 'great stink' (as they called it) outdoors, nothing could be done however. So powerful was the stench borne along on the Thames, that it actually enforced a closure of Parliament one summer in the mid-1850s – a significant achievement shared in history only by Oliver Cromwell and the Luftwaffe.

Filth, then, emerges as the true villain of *Bleak House*, surpassing the evils of the sadistic lawyer Tulkinghorn, or the homicidal Hortense, the insectoid stalker Guppy, or the vampiric Vholes. Specifically airborne filth, rising mephitically from the open sewers, from the 'nightsoil' (human excrement dumped in the gutters), and the animal droppings that caked the open streets. 'Mudfog' Dickens liked to call that poisonous atmosphere – for which read (and, with the mind's nose smell) 'shit-air'.

Why do the gentlefolk need streetsweepers like Jo in the world of *Bleak House*? Why does Esther mention 'pattens' – wooden clogs – in her description of the Jellyby house in Holborn? Step in a dog turd today and you will find the answer. Multiply that turd by a couple of million and you'll be reaching for your own clogs and a couple of coins for the zebra-crossing sweeper.

In April 2005, with great fanfare, the newly resurrected Dr Who went back, courtesy of Tardis time-travel, to 1870. Dickens allied himself with the doctor in his never-ending struggle against the forces of darkness. Inevitably, they won. The new

Plate 2. Cross-section of a lodging-house in Field Lane,
built over a sewer

Dr Who was charmingly done, although there was a very
poignant moment when Dickens (played with an eerie likeness by Simon Callow) asked the Doctor, as he returned to the
future: 'Will my books last?' 'Yes', the Doctor replied, as he
boarded the Tardis, 'they will last forever'. The Doctor could
of course have continued, 'but you won't, Mr Dickens: you'll
die of apoplexy (just like Sir Leicester Dedlock) within a couple of months'. But that would not have been very kind.

The programme was handled with a light touch, but it also

made an important critical point. Great writers create not just for their own time (1852–53, in the case of *Bleak House*) but for our time (2005) and – although only a Time Lord would know – for all time. But one thing was missing from Dr Who's Victorian fantasia – the *smell*. Everything we saw on the screen was too clean. The eyes enjoyed it, but the nostrils did not twitch. The BBC's adaptation of *Bleak House* will have failed if it does not get twelve million nostrils twitching.

This guide has been devised to assist the contemporary reader to fully immerse his or herself in the world of *Bleak House* – to view it (and, where mudfog is concerned, 'smell' it) as vividly as one does the other narrative soaps, serials, mini-series, and sagas we consume daily on our TV screens. It's a problem of common ground. The BBC's research and wardrobe departments (particularly the latter) are world class, but there are some areas of shared everyday experience that have been lost somewhere between the London of 1852 and the world that we live in today – gaps that even the BBC's wardrobe department cannot fill.

It is what we do not have to be shown on screen, rather than what the reader and viewer are shown and told, that is so significant. We share a world (even if we are from a different social class) with Ken Barlow, Dot Cotton, and Dev who runs the Corner Shop. In *Footballers' Wives*, our minds automatically fill in the blanks, connect the dots, do the invisible landscaping. We know, for example, although we are never shown it, what Conrad, Noah and Harley do on Saturday afternoons, we don't have to be shown it – unless it's strictly necessary to the plot (and in that epic bonkbuster, football never is). Victorians, for whom soccer was something played by middle-aged northern mill workers with droopy moustaches and even droopier pantaloons, would not know what was going on

Plate 3. The Fleet Ditch, showing the open sewers that
caused the cholera epidemics in London

outside the changing room doors at Earl's Park. They would
need to be shown, or have it explained to them.

On our part we don't know how, for example, Esther Summerson – her Dame Durdenish duty done – relaxes of an
evening (no TV but there is backgammon at Bleak House);
how she keeps herself clean and fragrant (Dickens is too much
the gentleman to investigate her toilette); what she eats for
breakfast; whether or not she reads a newspaper. Victorians
would know without having to be told. We don't.

We have not entirely lost Victorian England (more specifically, Victorian London), but there are gaping holes where that
distant country used to be. We know what a cobbled street

looks like, but not, probably, what a stream of metal-wheeled carriages clattering down one, the clatter intermittently muffled by horse droppings and straw outside the great houses, sounds like. We can imagine the gas or whale-oil lamps that lit the streets and some of the richer houses: but it's harder for us to visualise the strange aureole that gave them their distinctive luminosity. We do not automatically (since our street lights are automatic) factor in that romantic figure (about whom a contemporary of Dickens wrote a whole novel), the 'lamplighter'. 'You'd hear the patter of his feet as he came walking down the street, the old lamplighter, of long, long ago', as the popular song put it.

Excellent as they are, TV adaptations of classic Victorian fiction are always, for my taste, too brightly lit. There is, for example, a moment early in the story as Mr Jarndyce (perhaps foreseeing the ominous future) looks at Richard and Ada shortly after their arrival at Bleak House. Some way off Esther is watching all three of them:

> His look was thoughtful, but had a benignant expression in it which I often (how often!) saw again: which has long been engraven on my heart. The room in which they were, communicating with that in which he stood, was only lighted by the fire. Ada sat at the piano; Richard stood beside her, bending down. Upon the wall, their shadows blended together, surrounded by strange forms, not without a ghostly motion caught from the unsteady fire, though reflecting from motionless objects. Ada touched the notes so softly, and sang so low, that the wind sighing away to the distant hills, was as audible as the music. The mystery of the future, and the little clue afforded to it by the voice of the present, seemed expressed in the whole picture.

The candles have not yet arrived. The servants will soon bring them in. At this point of the day the Victorians, as they liked to say, would look for 'pictures in the fire'. It was fondly believed that the future could be seen in the flames and glowing coals – suddenly luminescent in the gathering darkness. This pregnant twilight moment – familiar to all Victorians – requires something less than modern high voltage – and something more. At such moments the reader's imagination, not the genius of Andrew Davies and Nigel Stafford-Clark, must get to work. Dickens's effect cannot be reproduced by studio lights, however artful. The aura surrounding Ada and Richard is an effect produced by a world in which light was a scarce and expensive commodity and used thriftily, even by those, like John Jarndyce, who were rolling in money. Masters of the house (as was their privilege) delayed calling in the candles for as long as possible. Nor were all candles the same. Those of lawyers' clerks, we will note, are 'fat' or tallow candles. They smell. At Bleak House, above stairs at least, they will be of wax, which does not smell as foul, but is expensive and, of course, gives a different, 'harder' quality of light and requires attention to the wick less often. In many of the night scenes, the characters should be carrying candles in the special hand-trays designed for evening passage through the house (there are no candles in the corridors). Half the scenes in *Bleak House* are night scenes. The reader/viewer must employ the mind's eye to stage them.

Hanging on the railings outside the Jellybys' house, we are told, there are milk and beer cans. Why the latter? Are these telescopic philanthropists boozers? The household drinks milk and beer because there is no supply of mains water, and that water available from the public street pumps (which served London's households) was highly dubious. On the north side of London, these public sources of water would be shallow wells. On the south side of the Thames, tidal ditches.

Plate 4. Miss Jellyby

There had been a devastating outbreak of cholera in London a few months before the publication of *Bleak House*. The disease practically killed Dickens's great rival, Thackeray, whose monthly serial in progress, *Pendennis*, had to be suspended while he recovered. Dickens actually saved Thackeray's life by sending his friend, Dr John Elliotson, to attend on him.

There were two theories of how the cholera was spread. The most popular was the 'miasmic' theory where poisonous air acted as the vector. From the introductory fog onwards, it is evident that Dickens inclined to the miasmic view. The alternative theory was that the disease was carried by water that had been contaminated by sewage, particularly by nearby cesspits. Dr John Snow was a main proponent of the water-borne theory. He proved his theory in 1854 (while *Bleak House* was still the book of the day) by vandalising the handle of the pump in Broadwick Street, serving the large population in

Soho. The cholera incidence in the area served by the outlet dropped instantly as the local population turned to beer to quench their thirst. Two monuments to John Snow stand in today's Broadwick Street – the pump, with its ceremonially broken handle, and the John Snow public house.

Middle-class families like the Jellybys, however disorganised their domestic affairs, and even if they were miasmically inclined, realised that there were dangers in drinking publicly supplied water. The colour and smell would have warned them off, if nothing else. Hence the children drank milk, the adults beer – or fluids, like tea and coffee, for which the water was boiled. At Bleak House, in rural St Albans, Mr Jarndyce's water would have been pure, the household served by a pump in the yard behind the kitchen, whose effluent would be crystal clear. In the Jarndyce town house, more care will be taken.

Can this kind of information be conveyed in a TV adaptation? Probably not. The six million viewers in 2005 will not see the Jellybys' beer cans, nor the Bleak House pump. The Victorian reader did not have to be shown them. There is more than one fog in *Bleak House*.

In London, the main sanitation problem then (as now) was how to dispose of human waste products. Rotting food, shit and corpses – to be blunt. Four years after *Bleak House*, Joseph Bazalgette began his great project to lay a huge sewage system beneath the city. His pioneering infrastructure purified London and Londoners still rely on it. If you want monuments to Joseph Bazalgette, look down the nearest drain.

The corpse problem took somewhat longer. One of the reasons that Dickens in *Bleak House* was obsessed with 'berryin' grounds' (as Jo calls them), was that they had become so overcrowded, and the paupers (many of them dying in cholera epidemics) were so shallowly buried that they were infecting the city's drinking water. One thinks of Victorian cemeteries as romantic places. In central London, they were anything but romantic. Dickens goes into Dickensian overdrive describing the graveyard (identifiably that off Drury Lane) when Lady Dedlock, with Jo as her guide, visits the last resting place of her lover:

> 'He was put there,' says Jo, holding to the bars and looking in.
>
> 'Where? O, what a scene of horror!'
>
> 'There!' says Jo, pointing, 'over yinder. Among them piles of bones, and close to that there kitchin winder! They put him wery nigh the top. They was obliged to stamp upon it to git it in. I could unkiver it for you with my broom, if the gate wos open. That's why they locks it, I s'pose,' giving it a shake. 'It's always locked. Look at the rat!' cries Jo, excited. 'Hi, Look! There he goes! Ho! Into the ground!'
>
> The servant [i.e. Lady Dedlock] shrinks into a corner – into a corner of that hideous archway, with its deadly stains contaminating her dress.

Plate 5. Consecrated Ground – Jo and the disguised
Lady Dedlock visit 'Nemo's grave

In the engraving he commissioned from Hablôt K. Browne for this scene, Dickens was careful to instruct that in the bottom left-hand corner there should be included the silhouette of a man drinking from a water jug. He too would soon be food for the rats. The problem of what to do with the unburied human residue of London – its daily crop of cadavers – was not solved until decades later when the cremation reform movement legitimised the burning of bodies.

Although not directly involved in the cremation movement, as he was in the sanitation movement, Dickens did play a major part in its development. He *created the climate* for reform, we may say. *Bleak House* was instrumental in the climate change that made London a better (or, at least, less deadly) place to live. If one wanted a modern equivalent to Dickens it would be, I suggest, the film-maker Ken Loach. But Loach, of course – for all the awards on his mantelpiece – is a minority taste – he fills no West End cinema. Dickens was, in addition to being a reformer, a writer for the people – a mass entertainer. Although some twentieth century critics saw this commercialism as Dickens's artistic Achilles heel, it was, in fact, the source of his extraordinary potency. He could address the masses and change their hearts and minds as no politician of the time could, and he seized the opportunity with both hands.

Victorians, rightly, saw Dickens not merely as a great entertainer, but as a force for progress. He wrote, as the Victorians put it, 'fiction with a purpose'. That purpose was to improve things – things outside the window, on the pavements, and in the streets of London. Hence his fury at 'telescopic philanthropy' – worrying about the souls of benighted savages in far-off continents when it was darkest London that needed attention. Hence the *j'accuse* in such moments as that when Jo finally succumbs to the 'deadly stains' among which he has passed his short, wretched life:

> Dead, your Majesty. Dead, my lords and gentlemen. Dead, Right Reverends and Wrong Reverends of every order. Dead, men and women, born with Heavenly compassion in your hearts. *And dying thus around us every day.*

You want to know how to make a better world? asks Dickens. Start in front of your nose. It is as appropriate a message now as it was in 1853, but you won't find that message in *Eastenders*. At this point, the soap opera and the Victorian novel part company.

One change for the better not even Dickens could bring about. The nose-offending fog that swirls, filthily, around the opening scene of the novel would swirl round London for a century more. It was not until the 'London Particular', or 'pea souper', wiped out thousands of London citizens in November 1853 (an exact century after *Bleak House*, it is morbid to recall), that the Churchill Government brought in the Clean Air Act. It could, as appropriately, have been called the *Bleak House* Act.

For the TV viewer and movie-goer, London fog tends to function as a device to evoke a romantic atmosphere. As the song puts it: 'A foggy day, in London town, had me low and had me down'. But there was nothing romantic about the fog that Dickens and the rest of London were obliged to inhale every winter. A couple of years before *Bleak House*, Thomas Miller (writing at Christmas in the *Illustrated London News*) described 'A London Fog' in terms scarcely less gothic than that of the first paragraphs of the novel:

> Such of our country readers as have never been in town about this season of the year, can scarcely imagine what it is to grope

their way through a thorough London Fog. It is something like being imbedded in a dilution of yellow peas-pudding, just thick enough to get through it without being wholly choked or completely suffocated … The whole city seems covered with a crust, and all the light you can see beneath it appears as if struggling through the huge yellow basin it overspreads. You fancy that all the smoke which had ascended for years from the thousands of London chimneys, had fallen down all at once, after rotting somewhere above the clouds; smelling as if it had been kept too long, and making you wheeze and sneeze.

A foggy day, that is, in London town (1853). It gets you down.

This guide aims to disperse some of the other kind of fog which has, necessarily, obscured our sense of mid-Victorian England; something that – for all its wonderful powers – a TV adaptation cannot do. As with any narrative dependent on an atmosphere of suspense, care must be taken against 'spoilers'. It is easy for the commentator to give too much away and that would be damaging. *Bleak House* is, as I have stressed, a 'social problem' novel. It is a melodrama – a 'weepy' at high points. It is what Carlyle would have called a 'Condition of England' novel, one that makes the nation look critically at itself, with a view to self improvement. Also among its richly innovative features, *Bleak House* is a 'whodunnit?' – arguably, with the introduction of Inspector Bucket, the *fons et origo* of the detective fiction genre. Part of the pleasure in reading the novel and watching its adaptation are those things that Dickens, teasingly, does not tell us. There is also, of course, that which the characters themselves do not know (who is Esther's mother? Esther wonders). Amazingly, Dickens himself often did not know what was coming next, as his working notes testify. He loved to let his novels work themselves out, 'writing to the moment' as he called it.

Bleak House was Dickens's ninth novel. He was, by this stage in his career, immensely artful – a master of his narrative instrument. He wrote all his novels in serial form – 'lisping in numbers' – which he preferred for a number of reasons, primarily because it brought him closer to his audience. Every month, he got a *feel* for the success of the story, not least by the monthly sales figures that his publisher, Bradbury and Evans, reported back to him. Readers would write to him, friends would discuss how the story was going – it was the most participatory kind of fiction. Narratives like *Bleak House* were phased to the monthly partition over a year and a half. In what follows, I have kept to Dickens's nineteen-part, rather than Andrew Davies' sixteen-part division. Although the architecture of the Page and Screen versions will be near enough symmetrical in their large outlines, Davies will have massaged the narrative into three fewer parts and excised much of the Dickensian bulk to force *Bleak House* into his televisual glass slipper.

Ideally, this companion should itself be used serially, to get some idea of the narrative's accumulating enigma, suspense and final set of elegant solutions (with a few dangling threads, about which we can only speculate – what, for example, happens to Esther's mother-in-law?). Ideally, too, this companion should be read more or less in tandem with the TV version. A summary, or running synopsis of the action, is given at the head of every part. Read ahead at your peril: you will be denying yourself a series of surprises. But, if you are the kind of person who likes to read the last page of a detective story first, so be it.

Bleak House: its place in Dickens's career and *oeuvre*

Bleak House is a pivotal novel, located in the middle of a writing career which began, explosively, with the *Pickwick*

Papers in 1836 and ended, mid-serial, and with Dickens still at the height of his powers with *The Mystery of Edwin Drood* in 1870 – at which point he was generally regarded as the greatest British writer since Shakespeare.

Plate 6. Portrait of Dickens, Herbert Watkins 1858

Like Shakespeare (and unlike most other writers), Dickens never stood still. Each of his major novels was, in some important aspect, an advance or variation from its predecessors. It was not merely his own career, but the evolution of the English Novel his genius was propelling at steam-engine speed. After an early phase in which, in his own graphic phrase, he nearly 'bust the boiler' (he had eight outstanding contracts for novels with various publishers at one point), he slowed his pace and began, after the mid-1840s, to plan his novels more constructively. Fascinatingly, the working materials (including those for *Bleak House*) survive, thanks largely to John Forster, Dickens's friend, biographer and unofficial literary agent. They are a window into his genius at the big-bang point of its creation.

Dickens could afford to take his time at this middle phase of his career. A major novel would yield him, nowadays, around £10,000. No other author, with the possible exception of Sir Walter Scott, had earned as much (and Scott died bankrupt: something that Dickens, who studied the Wizard of the North's career carefully, would ensure did not happen to him).

Bleak House is a carefully designed novel. It is also, like much of Dickens's later fiction, 'dark' in tone, and develops the 'social problem' aspect of his fiction (here the 'law's delay', as Hamlet called it) – something which he had pioneered fifteen years earlier with *Oliver Twist*, and would raise to its greatest height with *Hard Times*.

Bleak House is, as the Victorians called it, 'a novel with a purpose'. In the largest sense, it was to make England a better place. Specifically, the purpose was to do something about the scandal in Holborn of the branch of British Civil Law that dealt with the disposition of property. It is not, on the face of it, a sexy topic, although Dickens, with his usual supercharging, makes it seem like the one burning issue of the day. Every single abuse in the country – whether it be slum housing, smallpox, or the illiteracy of the lower classes – can be traced back to that old villain in his crimson and horsehair in the Court of Chancery; as much a fount of iniquity as the court of Nero. Of, course, as lawyers protested, Dickens exaggerates. But, as he would say, he who paints for the million must use vivid colours.

Despite his reforming 'mission', Dickens was careful – as careful as any soap opera serialist – to stress 'human interest' and, specifically, 'love interest'. As he wrote in his (postscript) preface: 'In Bleak House I have purposely dwelt upon the romantic side of familiar things'. Who will Esther, the humble, illegitimate housekeeper marry? This is the romantic question which gathers over the second half of the novel becoming almost as pressing a question as 'Who is the murderer?' or 'When the hell are they going to do something about that Court of Chancery?'

Accustomed as they were to love stories, Victorian readers felt a piquant novelty surrounding that word 'murder'. There was, of course, plentiful homicide in the traditional English novel (Gothic fiction is awash with gore). But with *Bleak House* Dickens did something quite unusual (for 1853); he stressed less the bloody crime (which we do not, in fact, witness), but rather the detection of the crime. *Bleak House* can claim, plausibly, to be the first 'whodunnit' in English literature. The perpetrator, of course, is ingeniously discovered by the sibylline Inspector Bucket – progenitor of Morse, Dalgleish, Rebus and all those other Police Department sleuths to be found on the 'Crime' shelves of Waterstone's.

Dickens's life

Dickens's life is a rags-to-riches story; the kind of fable that Samuel Smiles, the nineteenth century apostle of self-help, held out as a model to the young of the country. Dickens, as the Victorians liked to say, 'grew towards the light', proving that anyone could succeed. Charles [John Huffam] Dickens (1812–70) was born on the 7th February, 1812, at Portsea, the son of John Dickens, an £80-a-year clerk at the Navy Pay Office. Dickens's paternal grandfather had been a steward at Crewe Hall in Chester (which may explain some of the

Rouncewell–Chesney Wold plot in *Bleak House*). Dickens's mother Elizabeth was the daughter of a senior clerk in the Navy Pay Office who, in 1810, was exposed as an embezzler and who probably influenced a number of Dickens's characters. There were ten Dickens children, five of whom survived childhood. Charles (nicknamed 'Boz') was the eldest son.

Charles's early childhood was traumatically unsettled (a version of it can be found in *David Copperfield*). The family moved to London in 1816, to Chatham in 1817, and back to London again in 1822 to settle in Camden Town. John Dickens's salary (now around £350 a year), should have been adequate, but like Mr Micawber, he lived beyond his means. The home atmosphere seems to have been friendly, but neither parent gave the young Charles the intense love he craved. Nor, more importantly, were they good providers.

By 1824, the Dickens family had passed beyond penury into bankruptcy. Everything in the house was pawned and at the age of twelve Charles was put to work at a shoe-blacking factory on the south bank of the Thames (where the Hungerford footbridge now stands), at a wage of around 6s (30p) a week. Children were in demand – and relatively well paid – in factory work, for the nimbleness and dexterity of their little fingers. Although this menial labour lasted only a few months, the 'secret agony of my soul' was remembered for the rest of Dickens's life. As he told his confidant, John Forster, he would take lengthy detours to avoid that part of the Thames associated with his early trauma. Dickens could easily, with another push downward, have become another Jo (who probably does rather better than six shillings with his crossing sweeper's brush). The abyss was never far away.

In February of the same year John Dickens was imprisoned for debt at the Marshalsea Prison (an event which would resurface as the central plot element in *Little Dorrit*). Apart from Charles, the whole family lived with him there behind the prison walls, while little 'Bob' roughed it in lodgings in Camden. He discovered independence at an early age.

A small legacy enabled the family to discharge their debts by midsummer 1824 and Charles was sent as a day-boy to a decent London school. In 1827, however, the Dickens' finances were again precarious and Charles was articled as a solicitor's clerk in Gray's Inn, at something under £1 a week (rather less than Guppy earns with Kenge). He hated the law with a ferocity that can be felt, a quarter of a century later, in *Bleak House*.

Dickens, already a skilled penman, was attracted by journalism. He learned shorthand and became a Parliamentary reporter for the newspapers. A tincture of shorthand briskness carried over into his mature writing style. See, for example, the opening sentence (so-called) of *Bleak House*: 'London.'

By the early 1830s, Dickens was earning around £5 a week and writing more creative reportage for the newspapers. This led to his first success as a writer, *Sketches by Boz*, a series of snapshots of London that show Dickens, still barely twenty-five years of age, as an accomplished writer. Spectacular success (after a slow start) came with the *Pickwick Papers* which began selling in monthly parts (an innovative form of publishing that Dickens would practice for the whole of his novel-writing career) in April 1836.

There followed a string of hugely successful and original novels. *Oliver Twist* (1838), *Nicholas Nickleby* (1839), *The Old Curiosity Shop* (1841) and *Barnaby Rudge* (1841). These early novels show Dickens, in Thomas Hardy's vivid phrase, 'feeling his way to a method'. They cover all points of the fictional compass, from historical novel, through social problem novel, to melodrama – all laced with an exuberant comic style which was characteristically 'Dickensian'.

In 1843 Dickens broke more new ground with his pioneering 'Christmas Book', *A Christmas Carol*. But although his popularity was enormous at this time, the public reaction to *Martin Chuzzlewit*, published between 1843 and 1844, suggested that the readers might perhaps be tiring, or that they were simply glutted with his fiction. More importantly, Dickens might be overstraining even his formidable powers by writing so much, so quickly (a full length Victorian novel comes in at about three times the length of the average novel in 2005). There followed a lull in his writing during which he seems to have rethought the whole basis of his narrative art.

This new, more richly nuanced, accented and sombre middle period was ushered in by *Dombey and Son* in 1846, together with a cheap reissue of all Dickens's previous works – an action that enhanced his standing immensely. Towards the end of *Dombey's* serial run Dickens began an association with the banking heiress, Angela Burdett-Coutts and her Urania Cottage, a rehabilitation home for London prostitutes.

The serialisation of the autobiographical novel, *David Copperfield* (1849–50) earned Dickens his highest payment yet at around £7,000. Even higher sums were yet to come. At the same period he launched a weekly miscellany, *Household Words*, which became a primary outlet for his journalism. *Bleak House* was serialised between March 1852 and September 1853.

The pursuit of journalism perhaps explains a slowing down in Dickens's output of fiction. So too does his dedication to public causes (Administrative Reform, for example, a campaign highlighting the bureaucratic incompetence of the Civil Service in the wake of the Crimean War). Dickens was also heavily involved during the 1850s in amateur theatricals, with the aim of raising money for charitable causes such as the Guild of Literature and Art, to whom *Bleak House* was dedicated. These performances brought him into contact with the young actress Ellen Ternan (the 'Invisible Woman') who later, probably, became his mistress. The Dickens marriage had been unhappy for some years and the couple formally separated in 1858.

Little Dorrit was published in monthly instalments from 1855 to 1857. Two years later, Dickens relaunched his weekly paper *Household Words* as *All the Year Round*. The French Revolution novel, *A Tale of Two Cities*, appeared in its pages in 1859, followed by his second 'autobiographical' novel, *Great Expectations* (1860–61).

In 1858, Dickens had begun a series of immensely popular and remunerative public readings from his work in Britain and America which, together with editing *All the Year Round* (as well as his turbulent love life) absorbed much of his creative energy in the 1860s. Only two more full length novels were embarked upon: *Our Mutual Friend* (1864–65) and *The Mystery of Edwin Drood* (1870), which was cut short by his death in June of that year. In 1864, his health had begun to deteriorate rapidly with symptoms of gout and the early warnings of an impending cerebral stroke. In June 1865 he and Ellen Ternan were involved in a disastrous train crash at Staplehurst which shattered his nerves for months afterwards. His nervousness was sharpened by the fear that his liaison with the young actress might become common knowledge.

Despite all this and in defiance of medical advice, Dickens continued with a gruelling schedule of readings, including a triumphant tour in America in 1867 and '68, which earned him a satisfying £19,000. More important than the money were the emotional rewards of the readings, which were clearly hastening his death.

He died in the dining room of his house at Gadshill of a cerebral aneurysm on 9 June 1870 and was buried five days later at Westminster Abbey.

A Dickens toolkit

The only two essential tools for the understanding of Dickens's fiction are a good edition and a good biography. Fortunately, both are available: cheaply and in large quantity. Any of the standard, under £6, 'classic reprint' editions of *Bleak House* will serve. That in the Oxford World's Classics, edited by Stephen Gill, draws on the definitive 'Clarendon Dickens' text. Like the Penguin Classics edition, edited by Nicola Bradbury (with a new introduction by Terry Eagleton), it has the whole run of Hablôt K. Browne illustrations. Both editions are fully annotated. I have found particularly useful the Norton Critical Edition of *Bleak House* (1977), edited by George Ford and Sylvère Monod, which has 200 pages of most informative appendices. That will cost you a smidgen more than £6.

Of the many biographies of Dickens, two can be most usefully consulted: that by Dickens's alter ego, John Forster, published hot on the heels of the writer's death in 1870, and Peter Ackroyd's sympathetic *Dickens* (1990). Helpful guidebooks include the *Oxford Companion to Dickens* (1999), ed. Paul Schlicke, and Susan Shatto's *Companion to Bleak House* (1988).

There is a mountain of criticism and commentary on Dickens – most of it nowadays emanating from universities. Best ignore it until you embark on your PhD and enjoy the TV version instead.

*

Prefatory note: to maintain rough equivalence with the BBC's sixteen-part serialisation, I have followed Dickens's nineteen monthly parts, as issued serially from March 1852 to September 1853. A summary of each instalment is given, followed by points of interest arising in the number.

*

Instalment 1 (Chapters 1–4), March 1852

Summary

Dickens sets the scene with the first word (in fact the first sentence): 'London'. The novel opens panoramically with a shot of High Holborn at rush hour on a filthy day in November. Holborn Hill, a notorious black spot for Victorian traffic, is jammed. Fog swirls from the City streets, over Holborn's legal chambers and Inns of Court and down the estuary of the Thames, that artery via which London's commerce flows across the globe. There is a case in Chancery (the court of Equity) which has been continuing interminably for years – Jarndyce versus Jarndyce. No-one is quite sure what this internecine case is about (nor does the reader ever learn), but as part of its lazy deliberations, two orphans connected with the case, Ada Clare (a beautiful and cultivated young woman) and Richard Carstone (a recent graduate from Winchester School), have been made wards of court, and entrusted to the care of John Jarndyce, owner of Bleak House. Jarndyce's predecessor, Tom Jarndyce, committed suicide (a major hazard in this novel), driven mad by the 'case' and ever since, John has regarded it as the 'family curse'. It will be his mission to save his wards from the blight.

The scene switches abruptly to the country house of Sir Leicester and Lady Dedlock, at Chesney Wold in Lincolnshire. He is an aged baronet, excessively proud of his title and station in life. She is a reigning beauty, younger than her husband, haughty in manner, but with a mystery in her background. She is remotely connected with the case, although we are never quite sure how. The Dedlocks are served by the cold-blooded, hawk-eyed and sinister lawyer, Tulkinghorn. The attorney is interested to note that Lady Dedlock – normally ineffably bored – takes a sudden interest in a document shown her, relating to the Jarndyce case. As Tulkinghorn perceives, she recognises the handwriting of the scrivener who copied it and she is disturbed. Why? The lawyer will find out.

A second channel of narration opens up with the first-person narration of Esther Summerson. Illegitimate and on the verge of adulthood, she does not know who her parents are, but soon discovers that whoever they may be, 'Summerson' is not their name. She was raised until the age of fourteen by her 'godmother', Miss Barbary, a religiously strict woman whose severity Esther accepts with angelic equanimity, as she does the bullying of the only servant in the house, Miss Rachael. The young girl is meekly aware of her 'inheritance of shame'. She is, rather mysteriously, supported (it would seem) with remittances delivered via a London lawyer, Mr Kenge (known, familiarly, as 'Conversation Kenge', for the sleekness of his manners). When Miss Barbary suddenly dies (uttering ferocious Biblical imprecations against bastardy), everything is left to Miss Rachael. Esther is sent to boarding school in Reading, with financial support supplied through Kenge who informs her, mysteriously, that Miss Barbary was, in fact, her aunt. The financial support is from a complete stranger, Mr John Jarndyce, who evidently now intends for Esther to be his housekeeper (possibly, too, he sees in her a future mistress of his house).

After finishing at school, and now of age, Esther joins Richard Carstone and Ada Clare in London, where they are being disposed of by the Court of Chancery. They prepare for their trip to Bleak House, near St Albans, the home of John Jarndyce.

Before leaving, ominously, they meet Miss Flite, a decayed gentlewoman driven mad by the inequities and delays of the Court. Kenge has arranged that the three young people stay overnight in London with the Jellybys (recipients, like most of London, it seems, of John Jarndyce's inexhaustible largesse). Mrs Jellyby, the dominant power in the household (a reversal of the natural order of things that Dickens does not approve of) is an apostle of 'telescopic philanthropy'. Specifically, she devotes all her time fundraising and organising for the natives of Borioboola-Gha, on the left bank of the Niger. Meanwhile her own household goes to rack and ruin. Charity does not begin at home for Mrs Jellyby. Esther takes charge of the house, making some inroads into its Augean mess. She befriends Mrs Jellyby's luckless daughter (and slave-driven secretary) Caddy. Mr Jellyby has descended to a state of melancholy madness in a domestic *ménage* which, thanks to Mrs. Jellyby's 'telescopic' negligence, has descended into chaos.

*

Hooking the reader

With a serial, as Dickens knew as well as any circus huckster, you must hook your customer fast. In fact, his job was more difficult. A novel like *Bleak House* needed to be sold not once, but nineteen times. The trick was to secure what are now called 'early adopters' – as many as possible and then to hold on to them. For this purpose, the first 'part' was all-important. Passengers do not get on a moving train. Nor will they board one which does not, from the start, seem to be going somewhere interesting. A snappy, mysterious title was a useful device. Over the course of his career Dickens moved away from 'flat' labelling titles – like *Oliver Twist*, *Nicholas Nickleby*, or *Martin Chuzzlewit* – towards titles which were teasing and enigmatic – *Our Mutual Friend*, *Great Expectations* – and, of course, *Bleak House*. The novel's opening paragraph, arguably the most famous in Victorian fiction, is elaborately barbed with hooks. It is headed 'In Chancery', a legal term with overtones of 'chance'. It is also suggestive of imprisonment (caged birds recur as a leitmotif – although Dickens would not have used the term – throughout this novel). Thereafter, the paragraph explodes onto the page, scattering fragments of shattered grammar:

> London. Michaelmas Term lately over, and the Lord Chancellor sitting in Lincoln's Inn Hall. Implacable November weather. As much mud in the streets as if the waters had but newly retired from the face of the earth, and it would not be wonderful to meet a Megalosaurus, forty feet long or so, waddling like an elephantine lizard up Holborn Hill. Smoke lowering down from chimney-pots, making a soft black drizzle, with flakes of soot in it as big as full-grown snowflakes – gone into mourning, one might imagine, for the death of the sun. Dogs, indistinguishable in mire. Horses, scarcely better; splashed to their very blinkers. Foot passengers, jostling one another's umbrellas in a general infection of ill-temper, and losing their foot-hold at street-corners, where tens of thousands of other foot passengers have been slipping and sliding since the day broke (if the day ever broke), adding new deposits to the crust upon crust of mud, sticking at those points tenaciously to the pavement, and accumulating at compound interest.

If there is one word to describe this prose, it is urgency. Hurry, hurry, read on.

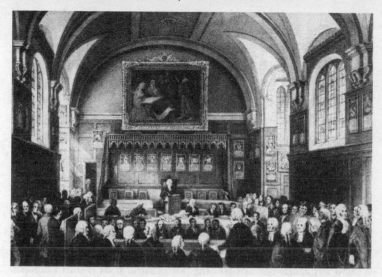

Plate 7. 'The Court of Chancery in Lincoln's Inn Hall',
by T. H. Shepherd

Why did Dickens call the novel *Bleak House*?

It was, as it happens, something that Dickens asked himself
rather obsessively. The all-important question – what should
he call this novel whose conclusion was some two years in the
future and which he himself had not yet decided upon? This
was not a small decision, after all, the title was the bait on the
hook, and he had to come up with one having written only a
fraction of the work. We can see from his preliminary working
notes that Dickens toyed with a string of possible titles. '*Tom-
all-Alone's*' (the mephitic slum in St Giles) was his first thought,
closely followed by '*The Ruined House*'. He then began to
consider using a 'mill' or 'factory', reflecting his increasing
interest in the industrial north: the workshop of England and
the world.

A building of some kind was clearly the focus of Dickens's

embryonic thinking about the new venture. He had, of course, himself just moved into a new house in Tavistock Square (it is, alas, demolished: although a blue plaque commemorates the spot on what is now the HQ of the British Medical Association). Dickens's previous novel had been named after its principal character, David Copperfield. What was appropriate for that work however, did not work for this. *Bleak House* was not, like its predecessor, a biographical novel, or *Bildungsroman* (another of the Victorian genres that Dickens could have patented). This new venture was to be panoramic – a 'condition of England' novel. There *is* no principal character (something, incidentally, which will cause problems for the TV adaptation). A central building, or symbolic structure, would organise the sprawling panorama, that much Dickens had worked out. But what should that central symbolic structure be? What 'ruined house' was Dickens principally thinking of? John Jarndyce's Bleak House near St Albans is certainly ramshackle and somewhat run down (until Esther takes charge) but it is hardly 'ruined'. Or was Dickens thinking of the dynastic seat of the Dedlocks – Chesney Wold – and the curse which will imminently bring the house down?

Dickens probably was not clear on the question himself. Other fleeting titular possibilities were jotted down on paper (many more must have fleeted through his mind). '*The Solitary House (that never knew happiness) … The Solitary House (that was always shut up) … Bleak House Academy … The East Wind … Tom-all-Alone's (Building, Factory, Mill) … The Ruined House That Got into Chancery and never got out*'. Finally Dickens settled on '*Bleak House*'. There would be no explanatory, or supplementary, subtitle of the '*Oliver Twist: The Workhouse Boy*' kind. He would, he decided, tantalise the reader. It would be a case of 'make 'em wait', and also, of course, 'make 'em wonder'.

What, for example, are we to make of the epithet 'bleak'? It implies misery – etymologically derived as it is from the word 'black' – but in common usage it has come to mean something more like 'unwelcoming', 'depressing', 'hopeless'. It is 'a dreary name', says the Lord Chancellor. Well said, my lord.

Of course John Jarndyce's house is, as we shall discover (after duly 'waiting') a rather jolly place; particularly when 'Dame Durden' takes charge of the keys. Bleak House under John Jarndyce's ownership and Esther's stewardship is anything but 'bleak' – or dreary. '*Cosy Corner*' would be as appropriate a name. The 'East Wind' – that bugbear of John Jarndyce's, signifying bad things to come – rarely blows over its roof tiles.

Dickens liked, as his plans make clear, to keep his options open as he wrote; never forcing his narrative where it didn't want to go. Like those who devise *Eastenders*' plot lines, he kept his story fluid, never planning, in detail, more than an instalment or two ahead. But, like all writers, he was thrifty with the fruits of his imagination. Dickensians will note that the 'solitary house that never knew happiness' is postponed to Miss Havisham's Satis House in *Great Expectations* seven years later. The 'Bleak House Academy' mentioned in the working notes resurfaces as Mr Gradgrind's school in Dickens's next novel, *Hard Times*, as does the 'mill town' theme.

For well or ill, Dickens finally settled on '*Bleak House*' as the title for his as-yet unwritten work. Why? Because, one suspects, it best suited the 'Condition of England' theme. English Literature is replete with works meaningfully named after country houses, from Andrew Marvell's *Appleton House* to E. M. Forster's *Howards End* and Evelyn Waugh's *Brideshead Revisited*. These houses embody 'England'; outlasting as they do any one set of owners, surviving through the generations,

enshrining the values and traditions that make survival possible. Given that tradition, Bleak House is oddly peripheral in
Bleak House's narrative design. Look, for example, at the cover
illustration to the nineteen monthly parts (it was the same,
from the first installment onwards):

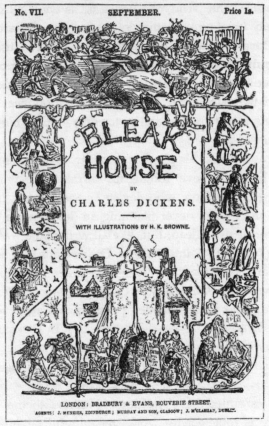

Plate 8. Cover of monthly parts of *Bleak House*

This vague representation of the house (the design commissioned in every detail by the author) witnesses to the fact that
when he began, Dickens was not entirely sure where his nar-

rative would lead him. The building features in the foreground (bearing no resemblance, in fact, to Dickens's later
description of John Jarndyce's residence near St Albans). In
front of this pseudo-Bleak House is Chadband, spouting ser-
monically as always (Dickens, one suspects, initially intended
to make the evangelical gasbag more prominent than he eventually becomes). No-one will get a solid impression of *Bleak
House*'s 'throughline' (as movie people call it) from this cover.

Compare this monthly cover with the frontispiece to the
volume edition of *Bleak House*, which was commissioned when
the novel was near completion and Dickens was clearly much
more certain of the shape and line of his work.

Plate 9. Frontispiece to the volume edition of *Bleak House*

The artist's style here is realistic (photographic, almost), not
cartoonish, and the allusions to written narrative are clear.
This is Jo, the street sweeper, about to be 'moved on'. Jo, we

may recall, is not present in the monthly cover design, but now – with most of the novel on paper – Dickens has all his narrative ducks clearly in line.

For those following the narrative serially, we have to wait, in the novel, until the second number (Chapter 6), until we are given a pen-picture of Bleak House. It is filtered through the naive and wholly provincial consciousness of Esther, who is seeing the property (which will be all-important to her) for the first time. It is worth quoting at length – emblematic as this building will be:

> It was one of those delightfully irregular houses where you go up and down steps out of one room into another, and where you come upon more rooms when you think you have seen all there are, and where there is a bountiful provision of little halls and passages, and where you find still older cottage-rooms in unexpected places, with lattice windows and green growth pressing through them. Mine, which we entered first, was of this kind, with an up-and-down roof, that had more corners in it than I ever counted afterwards, and a chimney (there was a wood fire on the hearth) paved all around with pure white tiles, in every one of which a bright miniature of the fire was blazing. Out of this room, you went down two steps, into a charming little sitting-room, looking down upon a flower-garden, which room was henceforth to belong to Ada and me. Out of this you went up three steps, into Ada's bedroom, which had a fine broad window, commanding a beautiful view (we saw a great expanse of darkness lying underneath the stars), to which there was a hollow window-seat, in which, with a spring-lock, three dear Adas might have been lost at once. Out of this room, you passed into a little gallery, with which the other best rooms (only two) communicated, and so, by a little staircase of shallow steps, with a number of corner stairs in it, considering its length, down into the hall. But if, instead of going out at Ada's door, you came back into my room, and went out at the door by which you had entered it, and turned up a few crooked steps

that branched off in an unexpected manner from the stairs, you lost yourself in passages, with mangles in them, and three-cornered tables, and a Native-Hindoo chair, which was also a sofa, a box, and a bedstead, and looked, in every form, something between a bamboo skeleton and a great bird-cage, and had been brought from India nobody knew by whom or when. From these, you came on Richard's room, which was part library, part sitting-room, part bed-room, and seemed indeed a comfortable compound of many rooms. Out of that, you went straight, with a little interval of passage, to the plain room where Mr Jarndyce slept, all the year round, with his window open, his bedstead without any furniture standing in the middle of the floor for more air, and his cold-bath gaping for him in a smaller room adjoining. Out of that, you came into another passage, where there were back-stairs, and where you could hear the horses being rubbed down, outside the stable, and being told to Hold up, and Get over, as they slipped about very much on the uneven stones. Or you might, if you came out at another door (every room had at least two doors), go straight down to the hall again by half-a-dozen steps and a low archway, wondering how you got back there, or had ever got out of it.

'Delightfully irregular' – gloriously ramshackle, wonderfully shambolic. If this is Dickens's Appleton House, or Brideshead, what are we to make of its 'irregularity'? He had, it is clear, contradictory views on the ramshackledom of England – a country which is the mother of modern democracy but has never codified, or even written down, its constitution.

Dickens would not have wanted it codified. He hated 'systems' (Mr Gradgrind's educational system in *Hard Times*, for example, which does to children what the treadmill does to prisoners). He loved jumble – his utopia would be the Old Curiosity Shop writ large. But another part of Dickens hated 'muddle' (see Stephen Blackpool's mournful refrain, 'It's 'aw a muddle'). Dickens particularly loathed muddle, as in

Krook's 'Rag and Bottle Warehouse' ('Bones Bought'), when that muddle was filthy, ugly, and destructive of the decencies of life (like the mounds of rubbish, veritable Alps of gunge, in *Our Mutual Friend*). He would be appalled, a couple of years later, by the 'muddle' of the British administration in the Crimea and threw his support into the Administrative Reform Association which would bring into being the modern Civil Service in the late 1850s.

Dickens, we may say, loved 'jumble' but hated 'mess and muddle'. He hated 'systems' but revered 'efficiency'. Did he contradict himself? Yes, like Walt Whitman, he contradicted himself. Truth can have two sides.

One thing is clear. The great house of England (Bleak House, that is) faces huge and imminent danger. It is lovely, but unless it modernises it will atrophy or die – like the Inns of Court (or the Houses of Parliament, the 'great cinder heap' as Dickens calls them in *Hard Times*). 'Reform' was a matter of urgency. But so was keeping the beautiful irrationality of England – the jumble of Bleak House.

The *Bleak House* weather forecast: implacable November weather

Unsurprisingly given the national climate, weather features prominently in English fiction. Usually bloody awful weather. One thinks of the sleeting rain in *Wuthering Heights*, the clocks striking thirteen in that bitter April (Eliot's 'cruelest month') with which *Nineteen Eighty-Four* opens. But few novels invoke the inclemency of the British climate more vividly than in the opening section of *Bleak House*. Look, again, at the opening paragraph:

London. Michaelmas Term lately over, and the Lord Chancellor sitting in Lincoln's Inn Hall. Implacable November weather. As much mud in the streets as if the waters had but newly retired from the face of the earth, and it would not be wonderful to meet a Megalosaurus, forty feet long or so, waddling like an elephantine lizard up Holborn Hill. Smoke lowering down from chimney-pots, making a soft black drizzle, with flakes of soot in it as big as full-grown snowflakes – gone into mourning, one might imagine, for the death of the sun. Dogs, indistinguishable in mire. Horses, scarcely better; splashed to their very blinkers. Foot passengers, jostling one another's umbrellas in a general infection of ill-temper, and losing their foot-hold at street-corners, where tens of thousands of other foot passengers have been slipping and sliding since the day broke (if the day ever broke), adding new deposits to the crust upon crust of mud, sticking at those points tenaciously to the pavement, and accumulating at compound interest.

Monthly serialisation meant that a story like Dickens's passed through one and a half cycles of the annual English seasons – everything from *Auld Lang Syne*, through *The Hazy Crazy Lazy Days of Summer*, to *God Rest ye Merry Gentlemen* and half way round again. Thackeray, Dickens's great rival, liked to synchronise his monthly parts with the current weather conditions (a habit he picked up from writing serials in the weekly magazine *Punch*).

Dickens didn't go quite so far as Thackeray in matching weathers, although he was careful, as in *Bleak House*, not to start a mid-summer narrative, for example, in midwinter. At a number of points, the narrative of the novel coincides calendrically with the weather patterns. The wonderfully fetid descriptions of London sweltering (unhealthily) in August in Number 6 (Chapter 19) of *Bleak House* was published – when else? – in August 1852.

It is the hottest long vacation known for many years. All the young clerks are madly in love, and, according to their various degrees, pine for bliss with the beloved object, at Margate, Ramsgate, or Gravesend. All the middle-aged clerks think their families too large. All the unowned dogs who stray into the Inns of Court, and pant about staircases and other dry places, seeking water, give short howls of aggravation. All the blind men's dogs in the streets draw their masters against pumps, or trip them over buckets. A shop with a sun-blind, and a watered pavement, and a bowl of gold and silver fish in the window, is a sanctuary. Temple Bar gets so hot, that it is, to the adjacent Strand and Fleet Street, what a heater is in an urn, and keeps them simmering all night.

And, if we look back, what do we find? It was a swelteringly hot August in 1852. Reading that Dickensian description with the heat of the day still on one's skin enriches response; one feels, as much as reads.

By November 1852, and the ninth number, narrative season and readers' season have again been exactly synchronised. The instalment (Chapter 26) opens: 'Wintry morning, looking with dull eyes and sallow face upon the neighbourhood of Leicester Square, finds its inhabitants unwilling to get out of bed'. Dickens's readers that month, wherever they lived (in that era before central heating, when bedrooms were ice boxes), would feel a familiar shiver as they contemplated the dash from the freezing bedroom down to the warmth of the kitchen.

The TV adaptation of *Bleak House* was scheduled by the canny BBC schedulers for Autumn 2005. Bigger audiences can be attracted after the 'days draw in', as the nation prefers to watch its televisions after darkness has fallen, but the choice of autumn was doubly appropriate, as the novel opens in November – 'bleakly'. His notes reveal that Dickens began writing *Bleak House* in November 1851, at the period when he was moving into his new (very unbleak) house in Tavistock Square – just a few hundred yards from that daily god-awful traffic jam on Holborn Hill which opens the novel. As he looked out of his window, across the Square, he must have thought – as do Londoners every November – 'God, another six months of this'.

November 2005 will be no exception, and the opening of Dickens's narrative, as staged by Andrew Davies, will move in harmony with the weather forecasts predicted on the BBC weather bulletin later that evening. 'Implacable', as usual.

Why is Dickens standing where he is at the beginning of the novel?

The opening paragraph (no need to quote it again) is narrated from a standpoint on Holborn Hill, the slope which – symbolically – marked a line between three great metropolitan entities: the City (the economic centre); Fleet Street (the newspaper and publishing centre); and Holborn (the legal centre). Holborn Hill, the main thoroughfare into the city from the East (now that there is a ring of steel around the city, it is once again), was a notorious traffic black spot. Dickens is viewing it at afternoon rush hour. As we will later learn, this street scene coincides with Esther, Ada and Richard's induction as wards of court, but the location never recurs in the narrative. Why does Dickens choose it?

Principally, one imagines, because it symbolised (although Dickens would not have used the word), 'gridlock'. Holborn Hill was a Victorian scandal, and was, as it happened, in the process of being addressed as Dickens wrote his opening paragraph – not by a congestion charge, but by one of the

Plate 10. 'Ludgate Hill', by Gustave Doré – gridlock

wonders of Victorian urban construction. Successful agitation throughout the 1850s led to construction in the 1860s, under the aegis of the Improvement Committee of the City of London (and at the almost unbelievable cost of £2 million), of the great Holborn Bridge and Viaduct, designed by William Heywood, and opened by Queen Victoria in 1869.

The Viaduct was (and still is) a noble structure; once seen never forgotten. It comprises a cast-iron girder bridge with three spans, and much ornamental ironwork. The whole is supported on granite piers, and framed by four Renaissance-style houses. The interior of the Viaduct contained a subway for gas, water and telegraph pipes, a passage and a sewer.

Staircases take the pedestrian down to Farringdon Road. The exterior was embellished by four bronze allegorical figures, representing Commerce, Agriculture, Science, and Fine Art (Law, alas, is excluded).

'Strike the Key Note', it pleased Dickens to instruct himself in his working notes. He chose this Victorian traffic jam as key note and overture to *Bleak House* because he, and his contemporary readers, would have seen Holborn Hill as metonymic of pervasive English inefficiency. The other targets Dickens tilted at in *Bleak House* – notably Chancery – withstood the novelist's satirical assault and reformist energies without the slightest change of their old ways. But Holborn Viaduct emerged as a magnificent tribute to mid-Victorian reformist zeal – assisted, one would like to think, by Dickens's pointed contribution. A reader of *Bleak House* in its late 1860s 'Charles Dickens' edition would, quite plausibly, have a dual vision of the opening paragraph: what Holborn Hill had once been like and what it was like now.

What's that dinosaur doing there?

Eastenders is one thing – *Jurassic Park* something else. Where did Dickens find his 'Megalosaurus' (a beast, alas, that will not make its lumbering appearance in the TV version) lumbering up Holborn Hill? Clearly the novelist is playing with the juxtaposition of traditional creation myths (primal soup, primal chaos) with, in stark contrast, the advanced urban, technological civilization of which the Victorians were so proud. One can, fancifully, see a premonition of Darwin's *Origin of the Species* (a book Dickens read when it first appeared in 1859). However, in the reference to the dinosaur in *Bleak House*, the Victorian reader in March 1852 would, inevitably, think of the

Great Exhibition of a few months earlier. Among the wonderful sights that all the world came to see at Hyde Park and its Crystal Palace in 1851, were the *papier maché* dinosaurs modelled by Robert Owen ('the father of modern palaeontology') in the 1820s, and sculpted by Benjamin Waterhouse Hawkins for the Great Exhibition. Holborn Hill is no more, but the monsters survive in Crystal Palace Park, South London.

Plate 11. 'Megalosaurus', from Richard Owen, *Geology and Inhabitants of the Ancient World*, 1854

This was the beginning of the popular idea of dinosaurs – particularly in the myth-making of children (who still love to look at the effigies in Crystal Palace Park). Dickens seems to despair that a country that can mount so magnificent a display of its technological genius to the world, can't get the traffic moving in central London. Little change in that department. A megalosaurus would still, on most days, overtake the jammed traffic at 5 o'clock on Gray's Inn Road.

Is the fog a 'symbol' or is it airborne excrement?

Dickens's second paragraph, with its rhapsody of fog, is one of the novel's best-known passages. But what, precisely, did Dickens understand by 'fog'?

Fog everywhere. Fog up the river, where it flows among green aits and meadows; fog down the river, where it rolls defiled among the tiers of shipping and the waterside pollutions of a great (and dirty) city. Fog on the Essex marshes, fog on the Kentish heights. Fog creeping into the cabooses of collier-brigs; fog lying out on the yards, and hovering in the rigging of great ships; fog drooping on the gunwales of barges and small boats. Fog in the eyes and throats of ancient Greenwich pensioners, wheezing by the firesides of their wards; fog in the stem and bowl of the afternoon pipe of the wrathful skipper, down in his close cabin; fog cruelly pinching the toes and fingers of his shivering little 'prentice boy on deck. Chance people on the bridges peeping over the parapets into a nether sky of fog, with fog all round them, as if they were up in a balloon, and hanging in the misty clouds.

Any teacher who has covered *Bleak House* with a class will be wearily familiar with the 'fog as symbol' essay, that informs the reader of the 'connecting' purpose of the swirling mist and its embodiment of the mystery at the heart of the plot. In actual fact, Dickens – routinely hailed as British fiction's supreme symbolist – would not have known a symbol had one been served up to him, roasted, on a silver platter for supper with greens and potatoes in his new house in Tavistock Square. Or, at least, he would not have known it by that 'French' name. The only mystery to him would be why these bright young A-level students and undergraduates who do him the honour of reading his story, decline to see the fog for what it is – airborne sewage. Atmospheric turds. 'Take a mouthful', he would have said, 'and then lecture me about symbolism – whatever that may be.'

Of course, like M. Jourdain, who was gratified to learn he had spoken 'prose' all his life without knowing it, an artist like Dickens can do things for which he himself does not have a handy critical term. When, for example, he writes: 'Thus, in the midst of the mud and the heart of the fog, sits the Lord High Chancellor in his High Court of Chancery', he does not mean that the great man is literally besmeared and obscured. This is, surely, figurative not realistic. Dickens, as the jingle puts it, is a poet and don't know it.

The fact is that Dickens's fog is not our fog – a much more wholesome commodity. This is the more important issue. He would not have sacrificed depicting the reality of this airborne pollution for the honour of literary effect, however grand. The fog in *Bleak House* was primarily *real*. More than that, it was poisonous – airborne sulphuric acid, distilled from a million coal fires, trapped by inversion and brewed into maximum toxicity. As one commentator put it, in 1855: 'sometimes it is of a bottle-green colour but at other times it is a pea-soup yellow'. Of course, an impressionist painter such as Pissaro (or Dickens's contemporary, Whistler) could see, with their artists' eyes, a kind of visual beauty in this, but for most it meant inflamed lungs, phlegm, and – not infrequently – death by suffocation. The BBC, with its trusty dry ice, will, of course, make Dickens's fog white – pure as driven snow. The opening scene will be moody, vaguely reminiscent of a house of horror. A foggy day, in London town, with sinister (and, yes, symbolic) overtones – nothing toxic.

One is glad that the watching six million won't know what Dickens was evoking in that second paragraph. The 'London Particulars', or 'pea soupers' disappeared from the metropolis in 1953 after a particularly horrible November in which thousands died. The Clean Air Act, passed through Parliament somewhat faster than its Victorian predecessor, effectively cleansed the city's winter air. If you want to know what Dickens meant by 'fog', ask someone who lived in the early 1950s, to tell the tale – not an A-level student.

One of the reasons that John Jarndyce is so vexed by the East Wind is, of course, that it tends to be bitterly cold (unlike the balmy south-westerlies). But there is another reason, for in London, the East Wind blew all the waste and debris from the docks, and the fish and meat markets at Billingsgate, Spitalfields, and Smithfield, directly into the West End, where the 'real people' lived (the Jarndyces and Dedlocks, for example).

Dickens's grammar and the Dickensian 'bounce'

Trollope, in his autobiography, has a chapter on novels and how to write them. In it, he writes: 'Of Dickens's style it is impossible to speak in praise. It is jerky, ungrammatical, and created by himself in defiance of rules.' No young writer, the Chronicler of Barsetshire warns, should model his writing on Dickens. The Great Inimitable should not be imitated.

Trollope was thinking (I think) primarily about the sentences of the first and second paragraph of *Bleak House*: 'London.' and 'Fog everywhere'. They are and they aren't sentences. Every primary school teacher, marking the day's literacy hour work, would wield the red pencil ('Grammar, Charles, Grammar!'). There is no verb, no subject and no object. Is 'London' a noun, a verb, an adjective? It is, one might guess, all three. Or a portmanteau into which all three have been somehow stuffed.

Writers have their characteristic energy. Dickens is high octane. One may remember that in his youth he was a shorthand writer and the habit of writing fast never deserted him. What these opening sentences convey, with their blithe violation of the canons of English grammar, is immediacy. It is almost as if Dickens is trying to dissolve language in his effort to communicate his sense of the amazing bustle of the greatest city in the world. And, again, he is hooking (too weak a term, rather 'harpooning') the reader who is pulled directly into the story. Suppose, for example, *Bleak House* began:

> Our scene, dear reader, is set in London, on a particular day in November. The year does not matter. Imagine yourself in Holborn, if you have ever been there. The inns of court – those hives of legal industry – are strangely quiet. The vacation, one of those many periods of rest that the guardians of our jurisprudential and legislative institutions require, such are their arduous labours, have begun. The weather is, alas, not good and the streets are muddy. But, recall dear reader, it *is* November. And not everyone in this vast metropolis is on vacation.

Dickens (unlike Thackeray, or the 'lesser Thackeray', Anthony Trollope) does not 'converse' with the reader. Instead he 'bounces' the reader into the text, a technique that is partly a serialist's device, but one that also reflects the characteristic qualities of Dickensian narration: speed and urgency. It also testifies to the extraordinary creative pressures that lie behind his novels. He first began thinking of the novel that would eventually become *Bleak House* in late February 1851, shortly after *David Copperfield* finished its triumphant serial run. He wrote to a friend describing 'the first shadows of a new story hovering in a ghostly way about me'. Something was 'haunting' him. Writing, for Dickens, would be above all else, an act of exorcism. In August 1851 he wrote to Angela Burdett-Coutts (the heiress who was his partner in the Urania Cottage Project, for fallen women): 'I begin to be pondering afar off, a new book. Violent restlessness, and vague ideas of going I don't know where, I don't know why, are the present symptoms of the disorder'.

What he describes is less 'inspiration' than a kind of creative madness – *furor poeticus*. It is this energy that propels and drives the narrative. Andrew Davies is expert in registering the characteristic pace and pressure of the classic writers whose texts he adapts. In *The Way We Live Now* he caught Trollope's gradual, but ultimately overwhelmingly massive narrative movement. In *Vanity Fair*, likewise, he captured Thackeray's characteristic variations of pace – its easy, clubman, conversational tone interspersed with sharp, ironic jumps. In *Daniel Deronda* Davies caught George Eliot's near-sermonical gravity. Catching Dickens will be like catching a non-stop express train as it hurtles past the platform.

Why does Esther pick up the narrative?

Dickens was among the most technically inventive of Victorian novelists. In *Bleak House* he uses multi-voiced narrative. The first two chapters are narrated, masterfully, by a Dickensian third-person narrator. Without warning, in the third chapter, the reader is surprised by the intervention (unprophesied on the title page) of a first-person narrator. Even more surprisingly, a very naive and, it would seem, somewhat imperceptive, narrator:

> I have a great deal of difficulty in beginning to write my portion of these pages, for I know I am not clever. I always knew that. I can remember, when I was a very little girl indeed, I used to say to my doll when we were alone together, 'Now, Dolly, I am not clever, you know very well, and you must be patient with me, like a dear!' And so she used to sit propped up in a great arm-chair, with her beautiful complexion and rosy lips, staring

at me – or not so much at me, I think, as at nothing – while I
busily stitched away and told her every one of my secrets.

His motives are baffling. Dickens, we may recall, had just
written one of the finest first-person fictions in English Literature in *David Copperfield*, and there was, following the
runaway success of *Jane Eyre*, a popular taste (particularly
among female readers) for 'I narrations' depicting the strug-
gles of young women in the world. Something along those
lines is predicted here, but unlike its predecessor, or Currer
Bell's (i.e. Charlotte Brontë's) bestseller, this novel is not entitled 'Esther Summerson'. Nor would it be an appropriate title
for the novel. *Bleak House* is more than one woman's journey
through life, although for artistic reasons which are clearly
thought out, that woman has a privileged position in the story.

As a narrator, Esther is sympathetic but not – as even her
best friends (and she will have many best friends) – would
claim, perceptive. She herself does not, for example, 'see
through' Harold Skimpole, Mrs Jellyby, or Deportment Turveydrop. But somehow we see through her naive account
what double-dyed hypocrites they are. It's a dazzling Dickensian trick.

The multi-voice narration device (which Dickens invents in
Bleak House) would be immensely influential. Wilkie Collins –
Dickens's *protégé* and one of the privileged group of friends to
whom Dickens read *Bleak House* aloud while it was in progress
– virtually built his career on the gimmick. Without *Bleak
House* there would have been no *Woman in White*, or *Moonstone*
(Dickens, ever restless artistically, never on his part used the
device again – bequeathing it, generously, to his 'sensational-
ist' disciples like Collins and Charles Reade).

One has to speculate. My speculation is that Dickens decided on a two-strand narrative in *Bleak House* because he felt that the sprawlingness of a novel with 'England' as its subject (rural, metropolitan, and, in its later chapters, industrial) needed 'anchorage'. More than that, it needed human interest; hence Esther's story.

Bleak House is as much 'A Novel Without a Hero' (or heroine) as Thackeray's *Vanity Fair*. It has a huge 'cast'; every instalment introduces, prominently, a new character (Virginia Woolf described it as throwing a new log on the fire every month, to keep it blazing). But no character 'owns' *Bleak House* in the proprietary way that David Copperfield does, with the first few sentences of 'his' story:

> Whether I shall turn out to be the hero of my own life, or whether that station will be held by anybody else, these pages must show. To begin my life with the beginning of my life, I record that I was born (as I have been informed and believe) on a Friday, at twelve o'clock at night. It was remarked that the clock began to strike, and I began to cry, simultaneously.

Esther's artless narrative is the glue that holds the massive design together. That is easily said, but it pertains to two big problems for the adapter of *Bleak House* for television. One problem is how to handle Esther's imperceptiveness so that we register it as imperceptive but see through it. Davies likes direct address to the camera, in the style of the Shakespearian soliloquy, to convey a character's interior thoughts (conversely he despises 'voice over'). The second problem is how to handle the multiplicity of *Bleak House*'s dramatis personae. The advertised cast list of the television adaptation runs to twenty or so. That of the first five numbers (counting major characters only) of the written text is twice that, and it grows with every successive number.

The economies of the TV serial with some 20,000 words of dialogue at its disposal, and a Victorian 'great baggy monster' (as Henry James famously called it) with half a million words, are very different. Economy will, inevitably, concentrate the viewing experience on a corps of central characters – Esther, principally. It's a question of quarts and pint pots.

Bleak House: the postcolonial dimension

In *Culture and Imperialism*, arguably the most influential critical treatise of the last twenty years, Edward Said, wrote that: 'Nearly everywhere in nineteenth- and early twentieth-century British and French culture we find allusions to the facts of empire, but perhaps nowhere with more regularity and frequency than in the British novel.' One might quibble about the rash generalisation, but, accepting, for the sake of argument, Said's universal law of Victorian fiction, where can we find the colonial–imperial dimension in *Bleak House*?

One need not to look beyond the first number. The first paragraph, with the City of London in the background and the second paragraph, with its passing reference to the 'tiers of shipping' in the Thames ports, sketch in the global–imperial reach of London. More specifically, colonial reference and arguably colonial critique is thick in the last chapter of the first number, which transports the reader to Mrs Jellyby's chaotic household. In her mania with 'telescopic Philanthropy', Mrs Jellyby, as Conversation Kenge tells the three young people who are to lodge (uncomfortably) with her:

> 'is a lady of very remarkable strength of character who devotes herself entirely to the public. She has devoted herself to an extensive variety of public subjects, at various times, and is at present (until something else attracts her) devoted to the sub-

ject of Africa; with a view to the general cultivation of the coffee berry – *and* the natives – and the happy settlement, on the banks of the African rivers, of our superabundant home population.'

It is, abstractly, an elegant scheme. Remove the human surplus to where it won't be obnoxious to middle-class sensibilities. The vagrants who clutter the streets of London (like Jo, when we later encounter him, or the brickmaker and his family) will be 'transported' far from the eyes of unsympathetic members of 'civilized' society, just as the convicts are currently (this being the 1830s) being shipped off to Australasia. 'Unemployed', 'criminal' – what's the difference?

As the Jellyby scheme gets off the ground there will be, in this African utopia, 'a hundred and fifty to two hundred healthy families cultivating coffee and educating the natives of Borioboola-Gha, on the left bank of the Niger.' Who, one may ask, is the coffee for? Are the natives going to sit, at sunset, by the banks of their great river, serenely sipping their double short lattés and Americanos? The Jellybys, the narrative is careful to note, drink coffee themselves. Indeed, Mrs Jellyby swills the stuff in huge quantities to keep her philanthropic energies up. 'We left Mrs Jellyby among her papers drinking coffee', as Esther says, when (with relief) they take their departure for St Albans.

Without mincing words, those natives will be slaves (their souls having been saved for Christ), working under the lash of the enforced emigrants transported to oversee their labours. What Mrs Jellyby is projecting is not a utopia, but a slave plantation. Dickens stresses the point by means of Caddy Jellyby's repeated protestation (as she slaves away for her mother) that she will not be a slave. Others, subject to Mrs Jellyby's benign/malign scheme, will. And what will those natives be slaving for? Not their own prosperity or health, but for the greater luxury of the English breakfast table and a commodity which can be traded, profitably, across the globe to rich countries where the coffee bean does not grow, but the drink is popular. Mrs Jellyby – if not quite the lash-wielding Simon Legree of *Uncle Tom's Cabin* – is one of the overseers in that complex process by which black labour is converted into black coffee.

Written three years after the last of the Opium Wars, in which British gunboats forced China to import from India the drug they desperately did not want, one can see Mrs Jellyby as launching, in her little way, a coffee war (opium is, we may note, another colonial product prominent in the narrative of *Bleak House*. It is not an overdose of caffeine which kills Nemo).

Plate 12. In an atmosphere of Borrioboola-Gha –
Mrs Jellyby's philanthropy in motion

It's not what you know, it's what you don't know

In the mid-1840s, ten years into his writing career, Dickens made a great discovery. A novelist could manipulate his readers not by informing them, but rather by *not* informing them. He could even make use of downright disinformation.

One could add another to the list of instructions; Make 'em laugh; make 'em cry; make 'em wait; and make 'em *work*.

Bleak House opens with a grand panorama (as seen, Dickens fancifully remarks, from a hot-air balloon) of the nation's august law courts. Then in an abrupt jump (faster than any air balloon could manage) we are transported to the fashionable country house, Chesney Wold, the Dedlocks' 'place' in Lincolnshire. What is the purpose of this translocation? What is the connection? It is, we deduce (after thought) something to do with the Jarndyce versus Jarndyce affair. But what? Tulkinghorn the lawyer notes in passing that Lady Dedlock is alarmed by one of the documents relevant to the case, which he has brought her. He is interested, but at this point does not know why and neither do we.

Another jump takes us to Esther, leaving school in Reading to join the two wards of court, Richard and Ada, in St Albans, with a stopover in London. Why, one may wonder, has John Jarndyce adopted the trio? They have no direct link to him, or with each other. Other questions swarm around the extraordinarily blank account we are given of Esther's origins. Is she (like Richard and Ada) an orphan? Perhaps. Certainly we deduce from her *soi disant* mother's remarks that she is a bastard:

'Your mother, Esther, is your disgrace, and you were hers. The time will come – and soon enough – when you will understand this better, and will feel it too, as no one save a woman can. I have forgiven her;' but her face did not relent; 'the wrong she did to me, and I say no more of it, though it was greater than you will ever know – than any one will ever know, but I, the sufferer. For yourself, unfortunate girl, orphaned and degraded from the first of these evil anniversaries, pray daily that the sins of others be not visited upon your head, according to what is written. Forget your mother, and leave all other people

to forget her who will do her unhappy child that greatest
kindness. Now, go!'

And die! presumably.

Under British Law (a very cruel law) at this time, illegitimate children took the name of their mothers. Who, then, was
Esther's mother? Is there a 'Miss/Mrs Summerson' held in
reserve to be released into the narrative at the tactical moment? Why, as she says, is Esther's godmother, Miss Barbary
(is that *her* real name?) the 'sufferer' from Esther's 'disgraceful'
birth? Why has her goddaughter's 'inheritance of shame'
blighted the older woman's life? Why does she live so separated from the world, at Windsor, with only one servant?
When Miss Barbary dies, the lawyer Kenge, who deals with
her affairs (begging the question of why an expensive London
lawyer, rather than the local solicitor, deals with the modest
estate of a country spinster) drops, in passing, that Miss Barbary is not actually Esther's 'godmother', but her 'aunt'. Or, as
'Conversation' Kenge puts it with legal pedantry, 'aunt in fact
though not in law' (bastards not having any legal relation-
ships, other than that with the mother). 'You have no
relations', he tells Esther, but reveals nothing else about her
parentage. Esther is, it seems, an orphan after all. Or, perhaps
(as she herself later suspects) she is the illegitimate daughter
of John Jarndyce who, at somewhere between the ages of fifty
and sixty, would fit the bill. Is it Jarndyce, via Kenge, who pays
six years' worth of Esther's boarding school fees? Why, generous fellow that he is, would he do that? It seems a rather
indirect plan to hire Esther as a governess for Ada, who is the
more accomplished and better educated of the two girls. The
less generous Miss Rachael, Miss Barbary's sole inheritrix
(nothing left to the live-in god-daughter, Esther) makes it clear

that she will not part with a penny for Miss Summerson. We are left wondering as to why John Jarndyce has 'spied' on Esther over the years, disguised at one point as the gruff old buffer in the coach taking her to Reading.

We know relatively little about the pasts of Richard and Ada, but they are less central to the narrative. And we do know their relationship to John Jarndyce and the 'case'. Esther, it would seem, has no such relationship. But there is that peculiar exchange in the Court of Chancery when the Lord Chancellor observes 'Miss Summerson is not related to any party in the cause, I think?' 'No' replies Kenge in open court (the fact will be taken down in the record). The lawyer then whispers something mysterious to the Lord Chancellor. What does he whisper? Are we to suspect that Esther *is* somehow connected?

There are people, complete strangers, who do seem to know a lot about Esther. When the three young people call on Krook's rag and bottle shop, the parodic 'Chancellor' mutters:

> 'Carstone,' he repeated, slowly checking off that name upon his forefinger; and each of the others he went on to mention, upon a separate finger. 'Yes. There was the name of Barbary, and the name of Clare, and the name of Dedlock, too, I think.'
> 'He knows as much of the cause as the real salaried Chancellor!' said Richard, quite astonished, to Ada and me.

So may we be quite astonished. How does *he*, illiterate old villain that he is, know about the 'Barbary' connection? It is six years since the bigoted Godmother has gone to meet her Maker (a crueler god, by far, than Esther worships). Obviously Kenge knows more than he lets on, as does John Jarndyce, and Miss Barbary, and even, the rag and bottle man. Why doesn't Esther know more than she does? Why don't we?

Plate 13. The Lord Chancellor copies from Memory

The working reader/viewer will put two and two together and come up with the usual fives. Many more questions arise in the first number, such as the reason for Lady Dedlock's dismay at coming across the handwriting of an unknown London clerk. We are told that her only 'part' in Jarndyce versus Jarndyce was her ownership of the property she brought to Sir Leicester when they wed. He married her for love, we are told. What, then, is *her* story? Why, is the Dedlock Estate lawyer, Tulkinghorn (who knows everything there is to know) ignorant, as he evidently is, of Lady Dedlock's maiden and Christian names? Like Nemo (as Captain Hawdon chooses to name himself), she is 'no-one'.

And just what is the Jarndyce versus Jarndyce case? It is one of the great vacuums at the heart of *Bleak House*, that we never quite know what the great lawsuit is about. Nor, evidently, do the lawyers. Or, perhaps, they will not say. Questions, questions.

What, historically, is *Bleak House*'s 'now'?

One of the problems in our twenty-first century approach to 'Victorian fiction' is the fact that the term 'Victorian' is a very blunt instrument. To say that the action of *Bleak House* is set in the Victorian Period is telling us very little. Finer calibrations than that queenly adjective are required. The 1840s and the 1860s are different worlds; as different as the 1940s and the 1960s were from one another. Looking back we blur such distinctions. Queen Victoria came to the throne in 1837 as a plump little girl. She died a fat old empress in 1901. Everything in-between those dates is, for our purposes of literary criticism, one-size-fits-all 'Victorian': bustles, corsets, beards, barrel organs, and drapes around piano legs.

Dickens, as readers of *Bleak House* would immediately have perceived, habitually 'antedated' his narratives, setting them in the past, often at the period of his youth. One notes, for example, that Esther travels by 'stage coach' from Windsor to Reading. She is fourteen, some six years before the 'now' of the narrative. There were, in 1852 as Dickens wrote and his readers read, perfectly good rail connections between those places. By mid-century, stage coaches belonged with the megalosaurus.

Other sections of the novel seem firmly in the present. Mrs Jellyby, for example, dispatches 5,000 copies of her Borioboola Gha circulars from the local post office. You could not do that until the early 1840s, after the Rowland Hill reforms in the national postal service, bringing about an era of modern communications of which mid-Victorians were intensely, and rightly, proud. Later in the narrative there is a reference to the telegraph – a facility not available until a year or two before *Bleak House*'s publication. Inspector Bucket will, we are told, soon be able to travel by train to Lincolnshire, although the service actually only opened in 1850.

Most centrally, in the depiction of Jarndyce versus Jarndyce, Dickens is clearly protesting against current, early-1850s abuses in the legal system. In his preface to *Bleak House* (published at the head of the volume edition, but in fact penned with the last serial number, in August 1853), Dickens writes:

> At the present moment there is a suit before the Court which was commenced nearly twenty years ago; in which from thirty to forty counsel have been known to appear at one time; in which costs have been incurred to the amount of seventy thousand pounds; which is *a friendly suit*; and which is (I am assured) no nearer to its termination now than when it was begun. There is another well-known suit in Chancery, not yet decided, which was commenced before the close of the last century and in which more than double the amount of seventy thousand pounds has been swallowed up in costs.

The case was, as the invaluable annotation to modern editions of the novel informs us, Day versus Day, a case begun in 1838 and still being heard in 1854.

Dickens's time slippages – which are ubiquitous in *Bleak House*'s narrative – create tricky problems for the dramatiser. Imagine if *Eastenders* switched, without warning or explanation (the characters not growing any younger or older), between the 1940s (when a pint of beer cost ten old pence, when meat was on ration, when no house had a TV, and mobile phones were science fiction), to 2005, mobile phones, beer at three quid, and satellite TV. That kind of switch seems often to happen in *Bleak House*. As I say, tricky. For us, that is. Victorian readers of Dickens clearly didn't have any problem with the story slipping and sliding through historical time like Dr Who in his Tardis. We do.

Don't you just hate Esther?

Dickens didn't. In fact, Esther is the great white hope in the novel. Wherever Dame Durden goes, she brings order, charity and goodness in her train – she drops cleanliness as promiscuously as Mrs Pardiggle drops evangelical tracts (and to much better effect). And, to add to her virtues, Esther is (unlike the Pardiggle and Jellyby women) 'submissive'. She, more appropriately than Pecksniff's daughter, might be called 'Charity'. But Esther is also an embodiment of the truth that charity begins at home. Dickens based Esther, as biographers have plausibly surmised, on his loved and admired sister-in-law, Georgina Hogarth, who looked as efficiently after the Charles Dickens household as Esther comes to look after John Jarndyce's.

Dickens practiced what he preached. In the Urania Cottage establishment, fallen girls were taught household skills (cooking, sewing, basic literacy, how to dress and clean themselves), before being shipped off to the colonies where there was a chronic shortage of wives (though no shortage of fallen women), for the men who were building the British Empire. Dickens's policy worked. It is Esther (civilising the street girl little Charley, for example) who proves to be the true philanthropist. There is nothing telescopic about Miss Summerson.

Admirable as Dickens clearly thought this paragon of domestic practicality, it is hard for the modern reader to warm to Esther Summerson (almost as hard as to warm to Jane Austen's Fanny Price). She kisses the rod, accepting her 'disgrace' far too meekly. Consider, again, her first words:

> I have a great deal of difficulty in beginning to write my portion of these pages, for I know I am not clever. I always knew that. I can remember, when I was a very little girl indeed, I used to

say to my doll when we were alone together, 'Now, Dolly, I am not clever, you know very well, and you must be patient with me, like a dear!' And so she used to sit propped up in a great arm-chair, with her beautiful complexion and rosy lips, staring at me – or not so much at me, I think, as at nothing – while I busily stitched away and told her every one of my secrets.

Why won't she stand up for herself? Why does she accept so unquestioningly that she is 'different from other children'? It is not merely a Victorian obedience. What would Cathy Earnshaw (Emily Brontë's heroine) do? What would Jane Eyre do? They would, one thinks, resist.

It may be, of course, that underneath all that syrupy goodness, there is a tough little nut. As the novel progresses, Esther does seem – mysteriously – to rise to the top. The orphanbastard from nowhere becomes Mistress of Bleak House as irresistibly as Heathcliff, the orphan-bastard from nowhere, becomes master of Wuthering House and Thrushcross Grange. Is Esther's irresistible rise the reward for her inherent goodness? Is it the equivalent of winning the lottery? Or is there steel behind that demure façade, and a determination not to be done down?

Don't you just hate the Dedlocks?

Dickens did. He took his cue from Carlyle – the thinker who was most influential in the forming of Dickens's philosophy. The sage of Ecclefechan believed the aristocrats of his (and Dickens's) age to be 'unworkers', betrayers of the historical mission of aristocracy to lead and maintain a 'heroic' example. Britain's aristocrats embodied paralysis just like the Court of Chancery, which never came to a conclusion. They were useless and sterile – of archaeological interest only. It is no accident that although he married Lady Dedlock for 'love', Sir Leicester has not managed to beget any children by her.

Sir Leicester – a regency buck grown old – represents, like 'Deportment' Turveydrop, a legacy that the Victorians hated and wished to shake off. That legacy was epitomised in the dandyism and rampant immorality of Beau Brummell and the Brighton Pavilion. Sir Leicester, with his 'light grey hair and whiskers, his fine shirt-frill, his pure white waistcoat, and his blue coat with bright buttons always buttoned', is the Regency incarnate. His is a politically-inflected wardrobe. Such things resonated in 1852. Victorian dress had been politicised by Carlyle's first great treatise, *Sartor Resartus*, and its 'philosophy of clothes'. At mid-century, as Trollope liked to put it, that man or woman was considered best dressed whose dress no-one noticed. Sir Leicester, by contrast, dresses to be noticed. He is, after all, a person of note.

By the time *Bleak House* was published, 'decent' gentleman (Allan Woodcourt, for example), would be dressed in black suiting indistinguishable from that of funeral mutes. (Black clothes also had the advantage, of course, that they needed less laundering; hence their popularity with the impecunious lower middle classes, living in dirt-laden London.) The drab uniformity of Victorian male dress made a socio-political statement: 'We are not dandies' (thank God).

Is *Bleak House* a religious novel?

Religion poses a problem for the modern reader/viewer of *Bleak House*. Dickens went to church, believed in God, and wrote a life of Christ for Victorian children. The modern audience for his stories he would find steeped in an ignorant heathenism, unable to pick up the numerous religious signals his narrative contains.

There is, for example, a telling moment when Esther is 'almost fourteen' (the age of puberty in Victorian England, and when children were routinely 'confirmed'). She is reading the Bible to her godmother:

> It must have been two years afterwards, and I was almost fourteen, when one dreadful night my godmother and I sat at the fireside. I was reading aloud, and she was listening. I had come down at nine o'clock, as I always did, to read the Bible to her; and was reading from St. John, how our Saviour stooped down, writing with his finger in the dust, when they brought the sinful woman to him.
>
> 'So when they continued asking him, he lifted up himself and said unto them, He that is without sin among you, let him first cast a stone at her!'
>
> I was stopped by my godmother's rising, putting her hand to her head, and crying out, in an awful voice, from quite another part of the book:
>
> 'Watch ye, therefore! lest coming suddenly he find you sleeping. And what I say unto you, I say unto all, Watch!'

At which point Miss Barbary suffers a stroke, from which she later dies.

Most Victorian readers, drilled by years at Sunday School, would have picked up the drastically opposed quotations from the New Testament. The first, about casting the first stone, is from John 8:7. It enjoins charity to the woman 'taken in adultery'. Miss Barbary's retort is from Mark 13: 35–7, alluding to the second coming and damnation for sinners. Miss Barbary would, as it happens, willingly cast the first stone (and as we later learn) has done so.

Which, the narrative asks, is the truer Christianity? Esther's gentle forgivingness to the sinner, or Miss Barbary's moral severity? As the novel expands, further options arise in Miss Flite's apocalyptic mania and Chadband's low church evangelism. When Jo dies, repeating the Lord's Prayer for the first time, can the modern reader accept (as Dickens's narrative clearly wants us to accept) that the little waif, unbaptised and criminal as he is, will be going to a better place? Reading/viewing *Bleak House* with a Victorian mindset is hard; with a *religious* Victorian mindset (such as Dickens requires) harder still.

*

Instalment 2 (Chapters 5–7), April 1852

Summary

Esther sets to and cleans up (what she can) of the Jellyby household. In so doing she makes closer acquaintance with the daughter of the house, Caddy, who is indentured as her mother's unwilling secretary, and promised in marriage to the unattractive Mr Quale. Esther, Ada and Richard meet Miss Flite again. She takes them to her lodgings (where the poor old lady keeps her flock of symbolically caged birds). They meet her landlord, Krook, the illiterate proprietor of a rag and bottle warehouse. They see, in passing, a card advertising copying services by a 'respectable man' (Nemo, as we later learn) who also lodges with Krook. Krook, it transpires, is familiar with the Jarndyce versus Jarndyce case, and recognises the young people (including Esther, strangely) by name. He himself is nicknamed 'the Lord Chancellor'. Like Miss Flite's caged birds, the title is meaningful. Krook relates the story of one of his former tenants, Tom Jarndyce, who, driven mad by the delays of the great case, blew his head off with a gun.

Having made their visit, the young people travel by coach to St Albans, Bleak House, and the care of the amiable John Jarndyce. A man 'nearer sixty than fifty', it is his crotchet to complain that the 'wind is in the east' when anything happens to upset, vex, or worry him. The wind frequently is in the east. He stands in the relationship of 'cousin' to Richard and Ada, and 'guardian' to the slightly older Esther. Esther stands in the relationship of 'companion' to the younger Ada. They meet Mr Skimpole – 'an elderly child' (in fact a shameless hypocrite, manifestly sponging off the guileless Jarndyce). When Skimpole, as happens often, is apprehended by bailiffs, Richard and Esther bail the humbug out. They make the acquaintance of the bailiff, Coavinses – an honest man in an unpleasant trade.

The action switches to Chesney Wold in Lincolnshire, where we learn of the 'Ghost's Walk' and the curse (emanating from a wretched marriage) that hangs over the house of Dedlock. We meet the housekeeper, Mrs Rouncewell, and learn of her two sons. One, 'the Ironmaster', has made his fortune in the industrial north. The other has run away into the army and his fate is unknown. The Ironmaster's son, Watt (meaningful name), is staying with his grandmother and has fallen in love with the village beauty, Rosa. The lawyer's clerk, Guppy (in the service of Kenge and Carboy), visits Chesney Wold and looks around the pictures in the long drawing room. He is very taken with a picture of the present Lady Dedlock which hangs prominently there. It reminds him of someone he has recently seen in London (Esther, it will emerge).

*

What garbage, precisely, does Krook deal in?

Krook's 'Rag and Bottle Warehouse' deals in all the waste of Victorian London; animal skins, human hair, bones, waste paper. Krook is part recycler, part waste-disposal service, part manifestation of the filth, garbage and excrement which soils London. His shop symbolises (as does he, in his character as 'Lord Chancellor') the offensiveness of the Court of Chancery. Krook also allegorises the worst of Victorian England; filthy, illiterate and capitalistic: 'Do you have anything to sell?' is his first question to the three young people.

Bleak House = madhouse: how many inmates are there?

Referring to Krook, Miss Flite (certifiably lunatic herself, as Richard has rather hurtfully observed in her presence) says he is 'M —'. Mad, that is. He is not alone. John Jarndyce, with his constant references to the East Wind seems a little touched – Obsessive Compulsive Disorder, we would say. Guster has lost much of her brain's function as a result of the gross abuse she suffered in the baby farm where she was abandoned as a child. The Man from Shropshire (Mr Gridley, as we later learn) has been maddened to the point of homicidal violence by the Court of Chancery. Tom Jarndyce, on his part, was maddened to the point of suicidal violence. Richard Carstone, sadly, will descend, fatally, into what the nineteenth century called 'melancholy madness' – depression (with hints of bipolarity; his gloom alternates with periods of irrational jollity, or euphoria). Mrs Smallweed the elder has dementia; Alzheimer's *avant la lettre*.

Many characters in *Bleak House* are 'M —', as poor, mad Miss Flite would say. Enough, certainly, to fill a bleak house. What, for Dickens, defined madness? He alludes, in the sixth chapter of the number, to Pope's couplet:

> The ruling passion, be it what it will.
> The ruling passion conquers reason still.

Dickens's unhinged characters all tend to have such a ruling passion (or, in Jonsonian terms, a dominant 'humour'). With reference to John Jarndyce, the novelist uses a technical term (taken from the French psychologist, Esquirol) 'monomania' – his characters, that is, tend to be mad in one area of their lives

Plate 14. The Little Old Lady – mad Miss Flite

only. And, in the saddest cases, that monomania eventually infects the whole.

Dickens, at this period of his life, was friendly with John Connolly, the reforming head of Hanwell lunatic asylum. Like Connolly (as the depiction of Mr Dick in *David Copperfield* testifies), Dickens was a firm believer in the humane treatment of the insane. It was, by the medical practices of the time, a somewhat unorthodox view.

So *that's* why it's called 'Bleak House'!

John Jarndyce's house was traditionally called 'the Peaks', by virtue of its three-peaked dormer windows (see the monthly wrapper illustration, which – bafflingly – shows two). Tom Jarndyce, in the extremity of his mental derangement, changed the name to Bleak House and, true to the promise in the new name, let the establishment go to rack and ruin. John

Jarndyce explains the history of the house to the newly arrived young people:

> 'It had been called, before his time, the Peaks. He gave it its
> present name, and lived here shut up: day and night poring
> over the wicked heaps of papers in the suit, and hoping against
> hope to disentangle it from its mystification and bring it to a
> close. In the meantime, the place became dilapidated, the wind
> whistled through the cracked walls, the rain fell through the
> broken roof, the weeds choked the passage to the rotting door.
> When I brought what remained of him home here, the brains
> seemed to me to have been blown out of the house too; it was
> so shattered and ruined.'

Jarndyce has renovated the house, restoring its hospitable and cosy atmosphere, but has kept the name. Perhaps he will change it when (if it ever happens), the case comes to judgement.

The John Jarndyce enigma

John Jarndyce – the good fairy of the early numbers – is, on the face of it, the incarnation of kindness. He does not work, nor apparently has he ever worked. The only occupation he seems to have is playing backgammon for small stakes and dispensing charity to whomever needs it (and, as with Skimpole, to those who surely do not need it). He is a good age, and is spectacularly generous with his money. But where does that money come from? He is a nephew of Tom Jarndyce – who blew out his brains out and was, apparently, ruined by the case. How, then, does John Jarndyce contrive to be so 'warm', as the Victorians would say? We never know, although we go through the story wanting to know.

There are other things one would like to know. Has John Jarndyce (like his bosom friend Boythorn) ever been madly in love? Are there carnal designs in his adoption of Esther? Is he, one has to wonder, Esther's father? She herself so wonders – indulging 'shadowy speculations' that make her 'tremble'.

Jarndyce's own explanation for why he should have plucked Esther from nowhere, to be mistress of Bleak House, are unconvincing in the extreme:

> 'I hear of a good little orphan girl without a protector, and I take it into my head to be that protector. She grows up, and more than justifies my good opinion, and I remain her guardian and her friend. What is there in all this? So, so! Now, we have cleared off old scores, and I have before me thy pleasant, trusting, trusty face again.'

A couple of pages later we learn, to our amazement, that John Jarndyce is the proprietor of Tom-all-Alone's. This paragon of charity is a slum landlord:

> 'There is, in that city of London there, some property of ours, which is much at this day what Bleak House was then, – I say property of ours, meaning of the suit's, but I ought to call it the property of Costs; for Costs is the only power on earth that will ever get anything out of it now, or will ever know it for anything but an eyesore and a heartsore. It is a street of perishing blind houses, with their eyes stoned out; without a pane of glass, without so much as a window-frame, with the bare blank shutters tumbling from their hinges and falling asunder; the iron rails peeling away in flakes of rust; the chimneys sinking in; the stone steps to every door (and every door might be Death's Door) turning stagnant green; the very crutches on which the ruins are propped, decaying.'

It is very perplexing. Dickens does not pursue the link between Bleak House and the London slum, but the idea of

John Jarndyce grinding the faces of the poor while setting up as London's own Father Christmas is troubling.

Is Skimpole a child, a crook, or just a poetic soul?

If there is one Biblical Text which could stand, engraved in brass, over the whole Dickensian *oeuvre* it is 'except ye become as little children, ye shall not enter the kingdom of heaven'; closely followed by: 'But whosoever shall offend one of those little ones who believe in me, it were better for him that a millstone were hanged about his neck, and that he were sunk to the bottom of the sea.'

Dickens, like Wordsworth, revered the child as the species of human being closest to God. Children's deaths (Nell, Paul Dombey, Jo) scale the supreme heights of Dickensian pathos – pathos leavened with the consoling sense that these little strangers are returning, with minimum delay, to God's care.

Where does that put Skimpole who is, despite his middle age, 'a perfect child' as John Jarndyce calls him and as he himself constantly protests? Skimpole as we immediately apprehend, as Esther gradually apprehends, as John Jarndyce eventually apprehends, and as Richard never apprehends, is no child, but that blackest of Dickensian beasts – a hypocrite. Worse than that, he is an abuser (by neglect) of his own children. As Jarndyce tells Richard, who has enquired whether Skimpole has offspring: 'Yes, Rick! Half-a-dozen. More! Nearer a dozen, I should think. But he has never looked after them. How could he? He wanted somebody to look after *him*. He is a child, you know!' Dickens's hypocrisy-meter goes into the red zone every time Harold Skimpole makes an appearance in *Bleak House*.

Plate 15. 'We are not so prejudiced as to suppose that in private life you are otherwise than a very estimable man, with a great deal of poetry in your nature, of which you may not be conscious.' – the childish Skimpole

The savage depiction of Skimpole got Dickens into hot water. Affronted friends and knowledgeable observers of the London literary scene quickly recognised the depiction of Leigh Hunt (Keats's erstwhile patron). Dickens, as he customarily did, publicly fell back on the 'any resemblance is accidental' defense. But, in a letter of September 1853, he wrote:

> I suppose he is the most exact portrait that was ever painted in words! ... It is an absolute reproduction of a real man. Of course, I have been careful to keep the outward figure away from the fact; but in all else it is the life itself.

We of course, know little of Leigh Hunt (despite two recent biographies, both of which vigorously protest Dickens's satire). But thousands who knew literary London, AD 1852, picked up the likeness, and, doubtless, relished it.

Bleak House is the first detective novel. Who's the best detective?

Although, unlike Inspector Bucket (who will appear later), he has no badge, Willliam Guppy makes the early running as the sharpest sleuth in the novel. Kenge's observation that there is something strangely reminiscent about the portrait of Lady Dedlock hanging over the great chimney piece at Chesney Wold, 'by the fashionable artist of the day' (Samuel Lawrence?) inspires Guppy to put two and two together before any others in the action. On the basis of his shrewd deductions, and quick follow-up of clues, Guppy will go on to stalk one woman and blackmail another, while never making the mistake of falling foul of the law (he is, after all, a lawyer; if a lowly one).

Why are the Dedlocks cursed?

According to Mrs Rouncewell, the antique repository of Chesney Wold lore, there is a horrific legend attached to the Dedlock house in Lincolnshire, as romantic as any attached to the Tomb of Tutankhamun. It goes back to the Civil War (the closest that Britain has ever come to a revolution, the imminent prospect of which so haunts Sir Leicester). A difference emerged between the then master of Chesney Wold and his lady. He was a royalist, she supported the Parliament. To further the roundhead cause, the Lady Dedlock of those days was in the habit of secretly cutting the hamstrings of her husband's horses so that they could not serve the royalist cavalry. Her sabotage soon led to her being crippled herself by her infuriated spouse. She later died with the parting curse that she would haunt Chesney Wold 'until the pride of this house is humbled'. Her spirit haunts the Ghost's Walk in the woods, a reminder of doom to come. Is the present Lady Dedlock her vengeful predecessor's reincarnation? Will the roundheads (or 'Wat Tylers' as Sir Leicester likes to say) at last triumph in Lincolnshire, as the revolutionaries did in Paris in 1789 and 1848?

*

Instalment 3 (Chapters 8–9), May 1852

Summary

Esther is soon installed at Bleak House as plenipotentiary 'keeper of the keys'. She becomes acquainted with all the nooks and crannies of the sprawling place (most importantly, her guardian's 'Growlery', or den). John Jarndyce tells her about the house's background and how it fell into disrepair with the sad decline into madness of his uncle, Tom Jarndyce. John has washed his hands entirely of the case, regarding it as the 'family curse'. Esther performs her household tasks to perfection and is soon loved by everyone in the house, nicknamed, affectionately, 'Dame Durden' (after a character in a well-known folk song).

At Bleak House, Esther and her young friends become acquainted with Mrs Pardiggle, a rural equivalent of the telescopically philanthropic Mrs Jellyby in London. They accompany her on 'cottage visits' – one, that will be important later in the plot, to a brickmaker and his family. The brickmaker, an abuser of his wife and children, despises Pardiggle's religious tracts (which he cannot anyway read). Esther is characteristically kind to the brickmaker's unfortunate women, and their dying baby.

What, John Jarndyce, Ada and Esther debate, is to be done with Richard? He must be put to a profession – lest he fall victim to the Jarndyce curse. But what profession? It is a mark of Richard's amiable fecklessness that he is happy to give his small store of money to the parasite Skimpole – who is equally happy to take it.

John Jarndyce describes to Esther his particular friend (going back to schooldays), Lawrence Boythorn, who will visit them at Bleak House. A thunderously angry man who is, in actual fact, not angry at all, Boythorn's life was blighted by an unhappy love affair in his youth (take note, reader). He lives alongside Sir Leicester's estate, in a former parsonage at Chesney Wold. Boythorn and the Baronet are in dispute over a right of way, bordering both their properties.

Mysteriously, Guppy – the lawyer's clerk who visited Chesney Wold and was so taken with the portrait of Lady Dedlock – arrives to request a private interview with Esther. He makes a startling move, unashamedly going down on his knees and proposing marriage to the penniless, illegitimate girl whom he knows only by sight, and has met just once.

In Lincoln's Inn we are introduced to Snagsby, a meek, amiable law stationer who commissions copying work from Nemo, Krook's lodger. Snagsby has a hen-pecking wife (who suspects her innocent husband of having fathered every illegitimate child in London), and a servant, Guster, who is prone to unexpected fits. Snagsby supplies documents to Tulkinghorn, who is very suspicious of this man Nemo (who was, evidently, the scribe that copied the document which so excited Lady Dedlock). Tulkinghorn visits Krook's house, only to find Nemo dead.

*

What, in a word, is the first quarter of the novel 'about'?

The best single word would be 'Charity'. More specifically, how to administer charity. The Victorians had no welfare state, as such; only a parochial workhouse and hospital system, inherited (with Benthamite modifications) from the Elizabethans. Many of the principal characters in the novel are, necessarily, objects of charity, institutional benevolence (for what it is), or care. Richard and Ada are 'wards of court', their expenses paid by the Jarndyce account. The other orphan (Esther) is supported by her 'guardian', John Jarndyce, who is also financial patron to Skimpole, Mrs Jellyby and later, Jo. His direct and discreet benefactions contrast with the telescopic (and very public) charitable contributions of Mrs Jellyby and Mrs Pardiggle. If there is a proverb which sums up the early numbers of *Bleak House* it would be: 'Charity begins at home', nowhere more so than in John Jarndyce's home. Another charitable act appears later in the novel when Charley is taken on as Esther's servant, even though she is not, until Esther has brought her on, qualified. Snagsby, the kindest of the narrative's minor characters, is always ready with a half-crown for the unfortunates who cross his path.

Dickens was himself a shrewdly charitable man. With the help of the immensely rich banking heiress, Angela Burdett-Coutts, he set up Urania Cottage – an establishment that institutionalised Esther Summerson's philosophy, taking girls off the street, teaching them domestic skills (as Esther taught Caddy), and sending them off to the colonies on graduation to become good wives to lonely emigrants.

Where does Dickens stand on the question of women?

Dickens will strike the modern reader as sadly unreconstructed. The fact is, Dickens despised what we would call feminists (and what he, like Mrs Eliza Lynn Lynton, would have called 'the shrieking sisterhood'). His scorn discharges on Mrs Jellyby (a woman after Gordon Brown's heart), with her public missions and committees. It discharges even more venomously on (pre-feminist) Mrs Pardiggle, with her proud sexual assertiveness:

> She was a formidable style of lady, with spectacles, a prominent nose, and a loud voice, who had the effect of wanting a great deal of room. And she really did, for she knocked down little chairs with her skirts that were quite a great way off. As only Ada and I were at home, we received her timidly; for she seemed to come in like cold weather, and to make the little Pardiggles blue as they followed.
>
> 'These, young ladies,' said Mrs Pardiggle, with great volubility, after the first salutations, 'are my five boys. You may have seen their names in a printed subscription list (perhaps more than one), in the possession of our esteemed friend Mr Jarndyce. Egbert, my eldest (twelve), is the boy who sent out his pocket-money, to the amount of five-and-threepence, to the Tockahoopo Indians. Oswald, my second (ten-and-a-half), is the child who contributed two-and-ninepence to the Great National Smithers Testimonial. Francis, my third (nine), one-and-sixpence-halfpenny; Felix, my fourth (seven), eightpence to the Superannuated Widows; Alfred, my youngest (five), has voluntarily enrolled himself in the Infant Bonds of Joy, and is pledged never, through life, to use tobacco in any form.'

The lady's main offence is not that she has a protuberant nose, but the fact that she pokes it into the man's world. She does not know her place:

> I am a School lady, I am a Visiting lady, I am a Reading lady, I am a Distributing lady; I am on the local Linen Box Committee, and many general committees; and my canvassing alone is very extensive – perhaps no one's more so.

Plate 16. 'Alfred, my youngest (five), has voluntarily enrolled himself in the infant bonds of joy, and is pledged never, through life, to use tobacco in any form.'

Typically Esther (don't you just hate Esther?) advises Caddy to put down her pen (Dickens, as his treatment as editor of Mrs Gaskell suggests, did not entirely approve of women with pens) and pay more attention to Peepy's soiled linen. As a historical fact, Feminism in England mobilised itself around 'causes' and charity work – the kind that Dickens is so satirical about.

How, effectively, do the well-meaning middle classes help the poor?

One of the most violent scenes, from the social point of view, describes Esther, Richard and Ada's visit to the squalid brickmaker's cottage accompanying the do-gooder Mrs Pardiggle. Her distribution of tracts and uplifting homilies here is as useless as Chadband's efforts to preach to homeless waifs like Jo. The brickmaker is a brute – totally beyond redemption:

'Why, I've been drunk for three days; and I'da been drunk four, if I'da had the money. Don't I never mean for to go to church? No, I don't never mean for to go to church. I shouldn't be expected there, if I did; the beadle's too gen-teel for me. And how did my wife get that black eye? Why, I give it her; and if she says I didn't, she's a lie!'

Dickens was a realist. Like Marx he realised that there was a lumpenproletariat for whom you could do nothing and should not try – other than supply cleaner water so that they would drink less gin. But you can do something with the young women, like Jenny. It was precisely the procedure that Dickens and Miss Burdett-Coutts applied at Urania Cottage. They did not try to save the irredeemably corrupted women of the streets. Applicants were interviewed, to guarantee that they belonged to that corps of what Victorians liked to call 'the deserving poor'.

Where and how does Richard go off the rails?

Initially Richard is a wholly loveable character – a Herbert Pocket. Everyone likes him. He is well educated (by the standards of Winchester College at that period), cheerful and virtuous, but he fails one great test in life; the Carlylean edict 'work and despair not'. He runs the tinker, tailor, soldier, sailor gamut, sticking at nothing, in a spirit of Micawberism. Dickens, no less than Carlyle, believed in the doctrine of work. When in doubt, get busy – the devil and idle hands, etc. There are innumerable vindications of the doctrine in *Bleak House*. Take, for example, this paragraph from the sixth number. Esther has just returned from London and is vexed, perplexed and anxious, not about herself, typically, but about Richard:

If I could have made myself go to sleep, I would have done it directly; but, not being able to do that, I took out of my basket some ornamental work for our house (I mean Bleak House) that I was busy with at that time, and sat down to it with great determination. It was necessary to count all the stitches in that work, and I resolved to go on with it until I couldn't keep my eyes open, and then, to go to bed.

Work is not merely what we are on earth for, it is therapy. Sadly, this is a lesson Richard never learns.

How is it all connecting?

If there is a single passage which describes the complex coming together of the amazingly disparate elements in the narrative of *Bleak House*, it is:

What connexion can there be, between the place in Lincolnshire, the house in town, the Mercury in powder, and the whereabout of Jo the outlaw with the broom, who had that distant ray of light upon him when he swept the churchyard-step? What connexion can there have been between many people in the innumerable histories of this world, who, from opposite sides of great gulfs, have, nevertheless, been very curiously brought together!

Jo sweeps his crossing all day long, unconscious of the link, if any link there be. He sums up his mental condition, when asked a question, by replying that he 'don't know nothink.' He knows that it's hard to keep the mud off the crossing in dirty weather, and harder still to live by doing it. Nobody taught him, even that much; he found it out.

Dickens's novel could well have the same motto as E. M. Forster's *Howards End*, 'only connect'. Connection is not merely a matter of aesthetics. The context of the above passage is sinister (and derives from Carlyle's *Past and Present*). What connects the rag shop to the aristocracy? Their fine shirts, as Carlyle points out, are the product of sweated labour (the rag trade, as we call it). That sweat carries disease (aetiologically it probably wouldn't, but Dickens and Carlyle believed that it could). What were rags used for? Paper – the documentary litter excreted by Jarndyce versus Jarndyce. *Bleak House* starts as a veritable kaleidoscope. By the end, have no fear, it will be as intricately connected as a Chinese box.

Boythorn's bird and the universal cage

There are caged birds everywhere in *Bleak House*. Esther, going off on her first journey, takes one with her. Miss Flite has a whole flight of birds allegorising the iniquities of Chancery. Most surprisingly, the explosive Lawrence Boythorn has his caged bird, which he cares for tenderly:

'You have brought your bird with you, I suppose?' said Mr Jarndyce.

'By heaven, he is the most astonishing bird in Europe!' replied the other. 'He is the most wonderful creature! I wouldn't take ten thousand guineas for that bird. I have left an annuity for his sole support, in case he should outlive me. He is, in sense and attachment, a phenomenon. And his father before him was one of the most astonishing birds that ever lived!'

The subject of this laudation was a very little canary, who was so tame that he was brought down by Mr Boythorn's man, on his forefinger, and, after taking a gentle flight round the room, alighted on his master's head. To hear Mr Boythorn presently expressing the most implacable and passionate sentiments, with this fragile mite of a creature quietly perched on his forehead, was to have a good illustration of his character, I thought.

The caged bird is a powerful and recurrent symbol in English fiction (think, for example, of Lear's pathetic 'we two alone will sing like birds i' the cage'). Here they seem to have quite different values. One would, that is to say, rather be Esther's or Boythorn's bird than Miss Flite's.

Who was Boythorn's great love?

Boythorn, the loveable man whose bark is so much worse than his bite, has been marked for life by an unhappy love affair, as Esther's keen womanly eye perceives:

> I saw him so often, in the course of the evening, which passed very pleasantly, contemplate Richard and Ada with an interest and a satisfaction that made his fine face remarkably agreeable as he sat at a little distance from the piano listening to the music – and he had small occasion to tell us that he was passionately fond of music, for his face showed it – that I asked my Guardian, as we sat at the backgammon board, whether Mr Boythorn had ever been married.
> 'No,' said he. 'No.'
> 'But he meant to be!' said I.
> 'How did you find out that?' he returned with a smile
> 'Why, Guardian,' I explained, not without reddening a little at hazarding what was in my thoughts, 'there is something so tender in his manner, after all, and he is so very courtly and gentle to us, and —'

Well done Esther.

But who was the lady? At this point the narrative is congealing. There must be a 'connection'. But who *could* Boythorn (who was at school with John Jarndyce forty-five years ago) have loved? Jarndyce, like Dickens, does not say. Yet. Curiosity will remain burrowing in the reader's mind for some months more.

Why does Guppy 'offer'?

Plate 17. In Re Guppy. Extraordinary Proceedings

The obnoxious Guppy offers marriage to Esther, having seen the girl only once or twice before, and never socially. Why? He is not a romantic cove. The form of his proposal is comically legalistic, strongly implying that he has a motive other than his claim that Esther has struck a chord in his 'art'. Dickens lards the clerk's absurd offer with contempt:

> 'To proceed. My present salary, Miss Summerson, at Kenge and Carboy's, is two pound a-week. When I first had the happiness of looking upon you, it was one-fifteen, and had stood at that figure for a lengthened period. A rise of five has

since taken place, and a further rise of five is guaranteed at the expiration of a term not exceeding twelve months from the present date. My mother has a little property, which takes the form of a small life annuity; upon which she lives in an independent though unassuming manner in the Old Street Road. She is eminently calculated for a mother-in-law.'

It is all done, as the gent himself would say, 'according to form'. In one respect, however, Guppy is formally delinquent. He has not consulted Esther's 'Guardian', nor asked for permission to 'offer'. Why not? Because as a lawyer (what ever else, he can ferret things out) Guppy has ascertained that, unlike Ada and Richard, Esther is over 21 (just) and not a ward of court. Were he proposing to 19-year-old Miss Clare, permission from John Jarndyce, and the court, would be necessary. And out of the question.

What is going on? Why has Dickens given this ludicrous event prominence? Esther would no more marry Guppy than she would strip off her clothes and pole-dance for the company at Bleak House of an evening. The odious pettifogger knows something. But what? Does he assume she will inherit a fortune when the 'nearly sixty' Jarndyce dies. Has he learned (something that Esther herself suspects) that the girl is Jarndyce's daughter – the putative heiress? Would Dickens give such prominence to a character's preposterous act were it not connected to something big in the novel? No.

There is one other interesting feature arising from Guppy's offer and the accompanying statement of worth; namely the tiny amounts the 'genteel' lived on in the mid-nineteenth century – a hundred pounds a year, in Guppy's case (when Dickens was a solicitor's clerk, we may recall, he was obliged to get by on half that). If Snagsby gives Jo, the street urchin, half a crown, that is the daily wage of a 'respectable', almost professional, adult like Guppy, holding on by his fingernails to middle class status. Later, in one of Skimpole's rhapsodies, we learn that spring lamb costs eighteen pence a pound (the same price as Krook's favourite, top of the line, gin). As I write, in Tesco's, lamb is still under a pound a pound (gin, alas, has gone through the roof; although it's probably less explosive).

It is hard to be sympathetic with him but living a 'decent' life on Guppy's pittance is a daunting battle. He must fend for himself. How can he get that big step up to 'monied' respectability from shabby gentility? One cannot entirely blame him for going for the main chance.

*

Instalment 4 (Chapters 10–13), June 1852

Summary

Dickens introduces the mysterious 'Nemo' (or 'No-one'). Nemo is a scrivener of the kind Dickens had been in his youth, copying legal documents for a set fee per page. Nemo (we shall know him by another name, later) is introduced via a new character, Snagsby, the law stationer who employs his copying services (for a pittance). Snagsby, his hand always in his pocket for a half-crown to give away, is one of the charitable 'angels' in the novel.

We make a detour into the chambers of Mr Tulkinghorn, 'the Oyster of the old school, whom nobody can open'. He is meditating on the explanation for Lady Dedlock's interest in the anonymous copyist, hatching his schemes beneath an artist's depiction of 'Allegory' on the ceiling of his office. He is a lawyer at the top of the tree and the gulf between Tulkinghorn's wealth compared with the two-pound a week Guppys of Holborn is immense.

Nemo dies before Tulkinghorn can interrogate him about the document in question. Is it suicide? Opium overdose? Murder? An inquest is called in the nearby Sol's Arms, the description of which is a tour de force of Dickensian high style. It is revealed that a mysterious 'dark young man' – a junior member of the medical profession – was in attendance in Nemo's room and was presumably, the signatory of the death certificate. Jo the crossing sweeper is summoned to give evidence, although in the event he cannot properly testify due to his illiteracy, which in the eyes of the law, means that he does not qualify as a human being. That odd glitch is reported in the newspaper and later brings Jo into the centre of the narrative. The verdict is charitable, allowing Nemo Christian burial with a verdict of accidental death. Lady Dedlock has read the newspaper, and is still strangely excited (for one so chronically 'bored'). Tulkinghorn is, as ever, watching.

Among the other new characters we meet is Lady Dedlock's terrifyingly passionate French maid, Hortense. The great issue of what Richard is to do with his life is again raised and it is resolved that he will go into medicine. The residents of Bleak House accompany him to London (where there is an embarrassing encounter for Esther with Guppy at the theatre), to lodge him as an apprentice with the amiable Dr Bayham Badger and his formidable lady. Badger has a good practice in Chelsea. Among this medical set, Esther meets the dark young physician who attended on Nemo. He is very agreeable, but who exactly is he?

*

What should we make of Guster?

The Snagsbys' disabled servant serves no narrative purpose. She does, however, throw polemical light on the theme of charity. She is a 'charity girl', i.e. an abused, underpaid skivvy, working all the hours God made for fifty shillings a year (little more than Guppy makes in a week and the cost of two serialised copies of *Bleak House*). Like Smike, in *Nicholas Nickleby*, she was left brain-damaged by institutional cruelty. The maltreatment inflicted on her by the 'baby farm', or gothic kindergarten, in which she was dumped as an orphan (she was probably illegitimate) has left her suffering epileptic fits.

Guster (short for Augusta), is one of the host of harmless lunatics skirting the edges of *Bleak House*'s narrative, and is, along with Miss Flite, one of the most pathetic. She is 23 years old – about the age of those other orphans, Richard, Ada and Esther, and her plight weaves one of the dark fringes to Dickens's comedy.

Occupation writer

Dickens, as he never forgot, had once 'written for his life' as a 'penny a liner'. *Bleak House* the novel is dedicated to 'My Companions in the Guild of Literature and Art', a charity set up with another novelist, Edward Bulwer Lytton, to support writers and artists who had fallen on hard times (as most inevitably did, and still do).

It is no accident that Nemo is a writer – and, like Dickens, drives his pen hard. In twelve hours straight the scrivener copies '42 folio pages'. His rate of pay would be about a shilling a page: not bad, were he not in irregular employment and hopelessly addicted to opium. The worked-to-death writer is one of the more private images in *Bleak House*. Dickens was not thinking merely of the legal writers, but of all slaves of the pen.

Does Nemo kill himself?

Suicide hangs heavy over this novel. Tom Jarndyce, we have been told, blew his head off. Opium is discovered by Nemo's deathbed – has he made his final exit by self-inflicted overdose? He evidently used the drug as a stimulant ('The advantage of this particular man is, that he never wants sleep', Snagsby observes), and had been taking it for 'a year and a half' – long enough to know the limits of his tolerance and avoid making nasty mistakes. We may assume, therefore, that it is suicide. Charitably, as was usual in such cases, the 'Coroner's Quest' delivers a verdict of 'accidental death' so as to spare the corpse the barbarities inflicted in the burial of suicides (suicide being a capital crime).

Plate 18. Nemo

What can we make of Nemo's back story?

Nemo's life story is never entirely filled in, although the inquest reveals some tantalising details. The scrivener has not always been an addict and is, in fact, one of the charitable angels in the novel, being 'wery good' to Jo when he has coins to jingle in his threadbare pockets. He has undergone 'a fall in life', but while we know where he fails to (Krook's lodging), we do not discover where he fell from. Dickens stresses his age of forty-five years. Why? Tulkinghorn has rummaged, but been unable to find any papers in the dead man's room. They will, one suspects, turn up, but for the moment, the reader can only speculate.

Opium and gin

Nemo's drug of choice is opium, probably taken as laudanum (dissolved, that is, in alcohol). Krook's drug of choice is 'raw gin'. Both men overindulge to destruction. Both drugs were freely available and their distribution was neither controlled nor licensed. To paraphrase Marx, opium was the opium of the people, and Hogarth's Gin Lane had never gone away. Dickens seems to have no distinct reforming impulses in these matters being, seemingly, libertarian. Mrs Pardiggle doubtless would be of a different and more temperance-oriented mind.

Who is the 'dark young man'?

There is a young, unfledged, medical man of 'dark complexion' present, but not named, in Nemo's room. He appears again on the edge of the Coroner's proceedings. Why is he there? Dickens holds off identifying him, raising in the reader's mind the wild possibility that the dark young man might even have murdered Nemo. In fact, as we later learn, his name is Dr Allan Woodcourt and he is present at the inquest because he (charitably) attends on Miss Flite, Nemo's fellow lodger, and was called in when Nemo was found dead. His kindness to Miss Flite – and, as it emerges, to other penniless patients – endears him to Esther.

The coroner's inquest

There are various kinds of legal process in *Bleak House*, from the opening hearing in Chancery to the final murder trial. Most florid are the two coroners' inquests at the Sol's Arms. Suffused in sawdust, beer, tobacco smoke, victuals and spirits they become pure music hall, with entertainment provided by Little Swills, the comic vocalist who, like Sloppy in *Our Mutual Friend*, gives 'the Police-news in different voices' – and mimics everybody else as well. For all the macabre crowd-pleasing, Dickens evidently loved such spectacles. The law, that is, not as an ass, but a circus donkey. Scholars have identified one of the music hall songs that the raucous spectators at the inquest taunt the police with, 'The Workhouse Boy', who, unlike Oliver, gets rather more sustenance than he wants:

> To gain his fill the boy did stoop
> And dreadful to tell he vos boiled in the soup!

It is a version of Sweeney Todd's meat pies. Horrible, but horribly jolly with it. Jollier by far than the Court of Chancery.

Jo is a crossing sweeper. What does he sweep?

Jo is one of the utterly excluded in the world of *Bleak House*. He does not know his name. He cannot give evidence at the inquest because he does not meet the minimal test of competence: an ability to recite the Lord's Prayer (a social iniquity that Dickens publicized in one of his articles for his magazine, *Household Words*, a couple of years before, with respect to a street sweeper called George Ruby). Jo is more animalistic than any child in *Oliver Twist*. He lives in filth at Tom-all-Alone's and sweeps filth for a living. But what kind of filth, precisely?

If one follows the first paragraph, it is 'mud'. But, as Dickens would have pronounced it, the word would have had overtones of another of his favourite words, *merde* – shit. *Merde* was memorably compounded elsewhere into two of the author's most biting names, for two of his most shitty villains, Merdle and Murdstone.

As Fred Schwarzbach points out, in his book *Dickens and the City*, mud and *merde* had much in common in 1853:

> The mud of mid-century was, after all, quite different from the harmless if messy stuff children today make into pies. It was compounded of loose soil to be sure, but also of a great deal more, including soot and ashes and street litter, and the fecal matter of the legion horses on whom all transport in London depended. In addition, many sewers (such as they were) were completely open, and in rainy weather would simply overflow into the streets. Dogs, cattle in transit either to Smithfield or through the town (many dairies were still inside the city), and many people as well used the public streets as a privy, but then even most privies were simply holes in the ground with drainage into ditches or another part of the street. (London was still a good fifteen years away from having an effective drainage system.) The mud must at times have been nothing less than liquid ordure.

In other words, ugh.

The Dickensian churchyard

Dickens was of a mind with the reformers Edwin Chadwick and Henry Austin, that London's church graveyards were one of the city's greatest, and most poisonous, shames. Nemo, a pauper, is interred in a

> hemmed-in churchyard, pestiferous and obscene, whence malignant diseases are communicated to the bodies of our dear brothers and sisters who have not departed; while our dear brothers and sisters who hang about official backstairs – would to Heaven they had departed! – are very complacent and agreeable. Into a beastly scrap of ground which a Turk would reject

as a savage abomination, and a Caffre would shudder at, they bring our dear brother here departed, to receive Christian burial.

With houses looking on, on every side, save where a reeking little tunnel of a court gives access to the iron gate – with every villainy of life in action close on death, and every poisonous element of death in action close on life – here, they lower our dear brother down a foot or two: here, sow him in corruption, to be raised in corruption: an avenging ghost at many a sick-bedside: a shameful testimony to future ages, how civilization and barbarism walked this boastful island together.

Come night, come darkness, for you cannot come too soon, or stay too long, by such a place as this! Come, straggling lights into the windows of the ugly houses; and you who do iniquity therein, do it at least with this dread scene shut out! Come, flame of gas, burning so sullenly above the iron gate, on which the poisoned air deposits its witch-ointment slimy to the touch!

Dickens identified this burying ground as St-Martin's-in-the-Fields, at the corner of Drury Lane and Russell Street (nowadays one of the capital's prime tourist areas).

Like the sewers of London, the underground grave system of the metropolis was wholly overwhelmed by the masses sucked into London, the population of which was doubling every decade. Decaying corpses poisoned the water and the air in the vicinity. Dickens's assault on the interment scandal was one of the impulses that led to the legalisation of cremation (the rational disposal of dead bodies), twenty years later. Too late, alas, for Dickens himself who is buried, very decently, in Westminster Abbey.

Why, oh why, is Lady Dedlock so bored?

Boredom – Lady Dedlock's passionless ruling passion – is, we deduce, a front, or disguise. Behind the mask she is nervous and Dickens's hints as to why she should be so nervous are getting ever broader. For example, in Chapter 12, Chesney Wold is described, unwarmed by winter sunshine:

> Athwart the picture of my Lady, over the great chimney-piece, it throws a bend-sinister of light that strikes down crookedly into the hearth, and seems to rend it.

Bend sinister? Illegitimacy? Where is Dickens pointing us? My Lady sees Rosa, the village beauty, and asks how old she is. Nineteen, she is told. 'Take care they don't spoil you by flattery' she says, 'thoughtfully'. What, we wonder, happened to Lady Dedlock when she was that age? Behind the inscrutability she radiates mystery and glamour. For all her beauty (she is a Victorian pin-up, whose portraits are slavered over by the likes of Guppy), she was never on the stage. According to Mrs Rouncewell (who knows everything about the Dedlocks) 'My Lady has no family'. Nor has she engendered any. There are no children, (the purpose, surely, for which Sir Leicester married her). She is, like Nemo, from nowhere.

What is the significance of Boythorn's right of way dispute?

Boythorn is prosecuting a bad-tempered little lawsuit with Sir Leicester on the edge of the story, relating to a footpath. There is, however, a political dimension. Boythorn, as Sir Leicester astutely (and infuriately) perceives, is a leveller. 'Rights' (even petty rights of way) are anathema to Sir Leicester, redolent as they are of the Rights of Man. Like Deportment Turveydrop (whom we shall imminently meet), he deplores 'Levellers' – those who would dismember the fine old body politic of England. Sir Leicester advocates some judicious dismembering of his own:

'It is the character of such a mind, Mr Tulkinghorn,' Sir Leicester interrupts him, 'to give trouble. An exceedingly ill-conditioned, levelling person. A person who, fifty years ago, would probably have been tried at the Old Bailey for some demagogue proceeding, and severely punished – if not,' adds Sir Leicester, after a moment's pause, 'if not hanged, drawn, and quartered.'

There is no doubt where Dickens stands on the question of the past glories of the English constitution. In this number he introduces his scathing attack on 'Dandyism'. It is the cultural residue of George IV, Beau Brummel, and universal homage to the great god fashion:

Dandyism? There is no King George the Fourth now (more the pity!) to set the dandy fashion; there are no clear-starched jack-towel neckcloths, no short-waisted coats, no false calves, no stays. There are no caricatures, now, of effeminate Exquisites so arrayed, swooning in opera boxes with excess of delight, and being revived by other dainty creatures, poking long-necked scent-bottles at their noses. There is no beau whom it takes four men at once to shake into his buckskins, or who goes to see all the Executions, or who is troubled with the self-reproach of having once consumed a pea. But is there Dandyism in the brilliant and distinguished circle notwithstanding, Dandyism of a more mischievous sort, that has got below the surface and is doing less harmless things than jack-towelling itself and stopping its own digestion, to which no rational person need particularly object?

Sir Leicester and Deportment Turveydrop dress like the Regency popinjays they are. They are clean-shaven, cosmetically enhanced, and coiffeured. Dickens, like other Victorians of his time and class wore dark clothes, sported a shaggy beard and somewhat unkempt hair. Among all its other quests and causes, *Bleak House* is engaged in the great Victorian enterprise of redefining what it is to be a 'gentleman'. A gentleman, that is, of the preferred current style.

Plate 19. Deportment Turveydrop

What, do we deduce, are Dickens's politics?

Although no labels are attached, we may assume that Sir Leicester's politics are high (sky-high) Tory. 'Our party', as his starchily snobbish cousin, Miss Volumnia Dedlock, puts it, are made up of those hereditary placemen described in one of Dickens's angry satiric flights:

Then there is my Lord Boodle, of considerable reputation with his party, who has known what office is, and who tells Sir Leicester Dedlock with much gravity, after dinner, that he really does not see to what the present age is tending. A debate is not what a debate used to be; the House is not what the House used to be; even a Cabinet is not what it formerly was. He perceives with astonishment, that supposing the present Government to be overthrown, the limited choice of the Crown, in the formation of a new Ministry, would lie between Lord Coodle and Sir Thomas Doodle – supposing it to be impossible for the Duke of Foodle to act with Goodle, which may be assumed to be the case in consequence of the breach arising out of that affair with Hoodle. Then, giving the Home Department and the Leadership of the House of Commons to Joodle, the Exchequer to Koodle, the Colonies to Loodle, and the Foreign Office to Moodle, what are you to do with Noodle? You can't offer him the Presidency of the Council; that is reserved for Poodle. You can't put him in the Woods and Forests; that is hardly good enough for Quoodle. What follows? That the country is shipwrecked, lost, and gone to pieces (as is made manifest to the patriotism of Sir Leicester Dedlock), because you can't provide for Noodle!

Never let it be said that Dickens doesn't ride a good joke hard.

The Dedlock–Thomas Doodle faction represent government by inherited name, by nepotism, and by the kind of electoral corruption excoriated later in *Bleak House*. Dickens mounts a similar attack in his assault on the 'Barnacle' clan, who treat the Civil Service as a private fiefdom in *Little Dorrit*. There is no clear alternative offered at this stage of the novel, but we may assume that in politics, if nothing else, Dickens is in favour of 'reform' – the great issue of the time.

Why does Lady Dedlock have a French maid?

Perhaps the employment of Hortense was designed to vex Sir Leicester, for whom anything coming from across the Channel would bring associations of sans-cullotist horrors. More likely it is another of Lady Dedlock's ultra fashionable appurtenances. Hortense is from the south of France (an area Dickens by now knew quite well), and she is, like all those from her arid region, 'passionate'. She has been, we are told, five years in Lady Dedlock's service. Is this, then, how long the Dedlocks have been married? We are not otherwise informed. If so, aged now in her early forties, what was she doing before marriage? Again, we are not informed.

What are the decent professions?

As we know, Dickens believed devoutly in the Carlylean gospel of work. The most contemptible aspects of Sir Leicester and Deportment Turveydrop (those Regency relics) are that they are utter drones. They *do* nothing, except be themselves. Sir Leicester is paralysed by rank (and bodily paralysed by his 'aristocratic' ailment, gout). Turveydrop is similarly ossified by his devotion to 'appearance', or fashion. Drones, however beautiful to Skimpole (who is actually less a drone than a parasite), did not attract Dickens's admiration (his own work rate was phenomenal; he actually worked himself to death, eighteen years later – insisting on giving public readings against his doctors' frank advice that it would kill him).

The flashing warning signs over young Richard at this stage of the narrative revolve around his chronic inability to 'settle' to a line of work. There are a number of professions open to an intelligent young graduate from Winchester with a rich patron behind him: army, church and law, notably. Richard decides initially on medicine, but can't stick at it (he is contrasted in this respect with Woodcourt, a medical man without great talent who does stick to his task). Richard, we suspect, is developing an incurable optimism and a habit of living in the future, exercising a downright idle style of living. He is displaying, in a word, dangerous symptoms of Skimpolitis.

Dickens would analyse the syndrome at greater length, and much greater complexity, in his future novel, *Great Expectations*, where Pip (living in hope of his Jarndyce windfall), faces the same life dilemmas as Richard. There may have been a personal aspect to all this. Dickens, who had married young and imprudently, by now had children of his own coming into the Carstone–Pip danger zone. (Parenthetically one may note, as the dedication to *Bleak House* confirms, Dickens was, at this stage of his career, committed to raising the 'dignity of literature' – to make writing, that is, one of the decent professions.)

*

Instalment 5 (Chapters 14–16), July 1852

Summary

This instalment is set in London and opens with the introduction of a new character – another satirised hangover from the bad old days of pre-Victorian England – Deportment Turveydrop. A dandy and, like Skimpole, an 'unworker' (as Carlyle called them) Turveydrop is a devout worshipper of the (for Dickens wholly unlamented) Prince Regent. Esther makes Turveydrop's acquaintance through Caddy Jellyby, who is in love with the moth-eaten dandy's son, Prince. Caddy has rebelled against her mother's intention that she should marry the odious 'philanthropist' Mr Quale. Prince, a frail but loveable young fellow, supports his parasitic father by giving dancing lessons at Turveydrop's Academy in Newman Street. Esther takes to the young man and approves Caddy's choice. Under her tutelage, the formerly slatternly Miss Jellyby will make Prince a good wife.

Skimpole airily lets drop that the bailiff or 'follerer' Coavins (who was in the practice of 'taking' him for his chronic debts) has died. It is a matter of no importance to Skimpole, but John Jarndyce and his two girls call on the slum house where the bailiff's three children are left orphans, under the motherly care of thirteen-year-old Charley (Charlotte) the eldest. They also meet the maddened man of Shropshire, introduced in the first number, whose name we learn is Gridley. He has been impoverished and driven insane by the delays of Chancery.

Jo, the street sweeper, is living (or 'not dying', as Dickens puts it), at Tom-all-Alone's. Lady Dedlock (as we guess, al-

112

though she is not named) dresses as a servant to seek out Nemo's burial place, using Jo as her guide. She picked up his name in the newspaper reports of the inquest. The urchin takes her to the squalid burying ground where Nemo has been laid to rest.

At last we learn the 'dark young man's' name – Allan Woodcourt.

*

The mid-narrative sag

When Dickens felt his narrative was sagging (something that the pulsating month's sales returns quickly told him), it was his practice, as Virginia Woolf put it, to throw a new character on the fire to keep the blaze going. In this number he ratchets up the satire, with the newly-introduced characters of the Turveydrops and the Coavinses. Charley is introduced late in the number, for pathos and some strategic tugging at the readers' heartstrings. At this point in the narrative Dickens all but tells us what the connection is between Lady Dedlock and Nemo (no reader, surely, can be fooled, any more than Jo is fooled by the 'servant' disguise). But Dickens keeps the suspense taut by holding back the revelation of who Esther's father might be. Televisual serialisation generally dislikes introducing new characters with every instalment – different media, different rules.

Peepy's sheep: a footnote

When Esther, Ada and John Jarndyce call on Mrs Jellyby, Peepy, as usual, has gone missing. He is, it emerges, chasing sheep as they are herded along the street. It's a vivid little detail, filling in what for most viewers/readers will be a blank. Skimpole's favourite dish, we may recall, is eighteen-pence spring lamb. We know where it comes from today – the cold cabinets in Tesco – but Victorians had no refrigeration. Their table meat had to be (messily) brought into Smithfield's slaughter house and sold, still smoking, to the consumer. Peepy's sheep will not, for a certainty, appear in the BBC version. It is now summer in Dickens's narrative, and the droppings of animals (mainly the ubiquitous horse) will make London air scarcely more salubrious than it is in hellish, smoggy November. As one contemporary observer, Henry Mayhew, put it with overwhelming statistical precision in 1851:

> Concerning the sheep, I am told that it may be computed that the ordure of five sheep is about equal in weight to that of two oxen. As regards the other animals it may be said that their 'droppings' are insignificant, the pigs and calves being very generally carted to and from the market as, indeed, are some of the fatter and more valuable sheep and lambs. All these facts being taken into consideration, I am told by a regular fre-quenter of Smithfield market, that it will be best to calculate the droppings of each of the 1,617,300 sheep, calves, and pigs yearly coming to the metropolis at about one-fourth of those of the horned cattle; so that multiplying 1,617,300 by 10, instead of 45, we have 16,173,000 lbs., or 7,220 tons, for the weight of ordure deposited by the entire number of sheep, calves and pigs annually brought to the metropolis, and then dividing this by 4, as usual, we find that the droppings of the calves, sheep, and pigs in the streets of London amount to 1,805 tons per annum.

Go for it, Peepee! (And a small prize for any viewer who catches sight of a horse, cow, ox, or sheep dropping in the BBC's *Bleak House*.)

Why did the Victorians so hate the
Prince Regent?

We, two centuries on, have an affection for 'Regency' – fostered by our taste for Jane Austen and Georgette Heyer/Barbara Cartland-style romance. The word recalls Byronic bucks, empire bust-lines, ringlets and gowns. Victorian 'sages' like Dickens, Carlyle and Thackeray (most vituperatively) loathed 'the first gentleman in Europe' and the cult of fashion, conspicuous consumption, colourful dress, dandyism and moral recklessness that the Prince Regent fostered. This distaste makes an entry into *Bleak House*, principally through the Turveydrops. See, for example, Caddy's remarks to her moral mentor, Esther (the incarnation of anti-Regency):

> 'Mr Turveydrop's name is Prince; I wish it wasn't, because it sounds like a dog, but of course be didn't christen himself. Old Mr Turveydrop had him christened Prince, in remembrance of the Prince Regent. Old Mr Turveydrop adored the Prince Regent on account of his Deportment.'

Turveydrop lives for one thing only: to be admired; a man of fashion, a mirror of elegance. Dickens's narrative despises such a philosophy of life and discharges its lightning bolts on the absurd, superannuated dandy:

> a fat old gentleman with a false complexion, false teeth, false whiskers, and a wig. He had a fur collar, and he had a padded breast to his coat, which only wanted a star or a broad blue ribbon to be complete. He was pinched in, and swelled out, and got up, and strapped down, as much as he could possibly bear. He had such a neck-cloth on (puffing his very eyes out of their natural shape), and his chin and even his ears so sunk into it, that it seemed as though be must inevitably double up, if it

were cast loose. He had, under his arm, a hat of great size and weight, shelving downward from the crown to the brim; and in his hand a pair of white gloves, with which he flapped it, as he stood poised on one leg, in a high-shouldered, round-elbowed state of elegance not to be surpassed. He had a cane, he had an eye-glass, he had a snuff-box, he had rings, he had wristbands, he had everything but any touch of nature; he was not like youth, he was not like age, he was not like anything in the world but a model of Deportment.

Turveydrop shares with Sir Leicester a rabid hatred of 'levellers' and a terror of democracy. England, he complains, is in irreversible decline:

'What is left among us of deportment,' he added, 'still lingers. England – alas, my country! – has degenerated very much, and is degenerating every day. She has not many gentlemen left. We are few. I see nothing to succeed us but a race of weavers.'

Hablôt K. Browne's illustration shows him as a Prince Regent look-alike.

Plate 20. The Dancing School

Caddy's education – B+ in domestic science, A for effort

Mrs Pardiggle and Mrs Jellyby represent what Dickens hated in women – a promiscuous intrusion into the man's world, with their committees, subscriptions, and never-ending organising (and, he may privately have thought, writing novels, like that rather vexatious Mrs Gaskell). His ideal of womanhood is represented in Esther (Dame Durden, the lady with the keys, based on Dickens's dutiful sister-in-law and housekeeper, Georgina). As the novel progresses, Caddy and Charley take on Esther's admired, self-sacrificing characteristics. They, like her (and through her), develop into good women – angels in the house – who cook, darn, wash and keep the home homely. It is an excellent augury of future virtue that, inspired by Esther, Caddy practices her apprentice housekeeping arts on Miss Flite. As she tells her mentor:

'Poor Miss Flite! Early in the morning, I help her to tidy her room, and clean her birds; and I make her cup of coffee for her (of course she taught me), and I have learnt to make it so well that Prince says it's the very best coffee he ever tasted, and would quite delight old Mr Turveydrop, who is very particular indeed about his coffee. I can make little puddings too; and I know how to buy neck of mutton, and tea, and sugar, and butter, and a good many housekeeping things. I am not clever at my needle, yet,' said Caddy, glancing at the repairs on Peepy's frock, 'but perhaps I shall improve. And since I have been engaged to Prince, and have been doing all this, I have felt better-tempered, I hope, and more forgiving to Ma. It rather put me out, at first this morning, to see you and Miss Clare looking so neat and pretty, and to feel ashamed of Peepy and myself too; but on the whole, I hope I am better-tempered than I was, and more forgiving to Ma.'

Esther cannot but be pleased at her pupil's improvement.

Charley, too, who is a 'little mother' (a kind of Estherlette) to her two siblings, is educated into domestic proficiency by Esther. Without that education, what would she have done to support a family of three? She would, probably, have had to go on the streets. The point is made very specifically on her first appearance, that Charley is, as she protests 'over thirteen'. She has, as John Jarndyce notes, the body of a woman. Given that the age of consent at this period of the nineteenth century was twelve, it would have been the most feasible option for Charley to sell her woman's body. Prostitution would be a more profitable line of work (for a year or two, until that woman's body wore out), than juvenile washerwoman. Dickens had, presumably, saved many Charleys – as do Esther and John Jarndyce – through Urania Cottage.

Plate 21. Caddy's Flowers

Where, one enquires once more, does Mr Jarndyce's wealth come from?

The question of the source of John Jarndyce's money is one of the intensifying, nagging enigmas in *Bleak House*. Who or what is paying for the upkeep of Bleak House, its very wealthy master, and his many clients? Wealthy in himself, John Jarndyce is a never-ending flow of financial support to others. We now learn that among his many benefactions, via Kenge, he supports Miss Flite. Where does his charity end? More interestingly, where does the money wherewith he is so charitable, originate? John Jarndyce has no profession that we know of. The great case has, apparently, frozen the bulk of the family assets. Tom Jarndyce, from whom John inherited Bleak House, died penniless, apparently, leaving the property a ruin. The only possible source of income for the house's present owner that the reader knows of is, perplexingly, Tom-all-Alone's. 'Follow the money' is an injunction that does not work in *Bleak House*, for it leads nowhere.

So many orphans: what to do with them all?

There are enough strays by this stage of the novel to fill an orphanage. They include the three wards of court, Jo, the Coavinses, Rosa (in Chesney Wold) and Guster. Something must be done about them or bad things will happen. Dickens describes the bad things in a direct address to the reader, apropos Jo:

> Turn that dog's descendants wild, like Jo, and in a very few years they will so degenerate that they will lose even their bark – but not their bite.

It was Dickens's fear that England would, in fact, have its own 'French' Revolution – if not that of 1789, the 'second' French Revolution of 1848 (the 'year of revolutions' across Europe). Philanthropy is, as the Benthamites always argued, self-interest – help the destitute so that they do not rise up in protest against the conditions that oppress them. Caring societies are safe societies.

Plate 22. 'What's gone of your father and your mother, eh?' – Guster helps Jo

Lady Dedlock's horrible thought

There is an interesting moment as Jo is showing the mysterious 'servant' the graveyard where Nemo is buried. The gowned woman asks, in a spasm of horror, 'Did he look like — not like *you*?' What she evidently suspects is that Jo might be Nemo's illegitimate child. Why else would this drug-addicted, destitute hack be 'wery good' to this scrap of human offal, this outcast, this filthy, ignorant street urchin? It relates to a larger question hovering over much of the narrative. Who *is* Jo's father. The dedicated reader of Victorian fiction would recall a similar characterisation in Bulwer Lytton's *Lucretia* five

years earlier, where the illiterate street-sweeper urchin Beck
turns out, preposterously, to be the villainous heroine's long
lost son. By the melodramatic convention of Victorian fiction,
a revelation will be coming as, memorably, it did with the
workhouse boy in *Oliver Twist* and, as by now we can confi-
dently assume, it will with Esther Summerson.

*

Instalment 6 (Chapters 17–19),
August 1852

Summary

In this number, with his monthly readers safely on board, Dickens begins to dissolve the mystery – particularly the strange connection between Lady Dedlock and Esther (which the rat-eyed Guppy has discerned).

Some of the narrative fog is clearing. Richard finds himself temperamentally unable to settle down to his medical studies. John Jarndyce and the two girls visit him at his London lodgings with the amiable Bayham Badgers. He has, they have informed his increasingly troubled guardian (the East Wind blows keenly), no 'disposition' for doctoring. 'The law is the boy for me', he abruptly declares. With the long-suffering John Jarndyce's help, Richard is duly articled with Kenge and Carboy (dangerously close to the 'case', the influence of which is having a corrosive effect on him) and transferred to new lodgings at Queen Square (close to the Inns of Court).

On their return to Bleak House, John Jarndyce decides at last to inform Esther of what he knows about her background. She was, he tells her, entrusted to his care by a mysterious lady (ambiguously either Esther's aunt, or her mother), some nine years ago. The lady insisted on remaining totally invisible (another nobody). Esther apprehends, of course, that she must be illegitimate. But who, she continues to wonder, *are* her parents?

Allan Woodcourt, for whom romantic feelings are stirring

in Esther's breast (and in his for her, we deduce), has not prospered as a London doctor – probably because of his habit of taking on pauper patients like Miss Flite and later Jo and Jenny. Unlike Richard, however, and like the proverbial cobbler, he sticks to his last and goes off as a ship's surgeon to the East. Esther is warned off developing any romantic feelings towards her son by Allan's excessively snobbish (and excessively Welsh) mother – who wants no family alliance with a bastard daughter of nobody. Nonetheless, before leaving, Allan, a shy wooer, makes a meaningful gift of some flowers to Esther. She will treasure them. Ada perceives the direction Esther's heart is tending, although Dame Durden is too modest to admit it, even to herself.

Jarndyce, Skimpole and his two female wards make a trip (by coach – railways are still in the future, apparently) to see Boythorn, in Lincolnshire. His 'bachelor house' (formerly the parsonage) adjoins the estate of Chesney Wold, with its disputed footpath running between the properties. It is now high summer (as it is for the monthly readers of this number).

The Bleak House visitors stay over for the weekend and go to the Chesney Wold church. When she sees Lady Dedlock, Esther is overcome with a powerful, but inexplicable, surge of emotion. Her disquiet is compounded when they are forced to take shelter from a storm with the noblewoman. There is 'something' profoundly disturbing – and oddly familiar – in the great lady's face. By now, of course, the wideawake reader has worked out what it is. It emerges, from conversation while sheltering from the storm, that Lady Dedlock and John Jarndyce have known each other in the distant past, before she was ennobled. Lady Dedlock, the storm over, humiliates her French maid Hortense, by preferring the gentle Rosa over her. Hortense takes dismissal very badly.

The scene switches abruptly (as it customarily does) to London and the Inns of Court – sweltering in 'the hottest long vacation known for many years'. Only Snagsby and the clerks are left in town. Dickens introduces us to Chadband, the corpulent and gluttonous evangelical preacher who, when not stuffing food into his mouth, utters a stream of nonsensical sermonising from that same orifice. The Chadbands come to take tea with the Snagsbys (Mrs Snagsby is one of the Chadband faithful). Guppy is also present. Jo is brought in by a constable, who has charged him to 'move on' or be arrested for vagrancy. The constable is also suspicious about the sovereign that the mysterious 'servant' allegedly gave him. Jo recalls that Snagsby 'wos good to him' at the inquest, and pleads for his help, which the good-natured law stationer willingly gives. Chadband is notably uncharitable and gives only a torrent of sermon. It emerges (through Guppy's 'cross examination') that Mrs Chadband is acquainted with Esther. She is, we discover, Miss Rachael, Miss Barbary's hard-hearted factotum and inheritrix. More 'connexions'.

The number ends with Jo, sitting forlornly outside St Paul's, contemplating a destiny of forever 'moving on', until he joins Nemo in the 'berryin' ground'.

*

What do we know of Ada's back story?

We are told very little of Ada's story, although a few details rise slowly to the surface. When, by sheer goodness, she persuades John Jarndyce to acquiesce in Richard's reckless decision to give up medicine and become a lawyer (foredoomed, of course), he looks, carefully, at her, and (with biblical echo) declares:

> 'I think,' said my Guardian, thoughtfully regarding her, 'I think it must be somewhere written that the virtues of the mothers shall, occasionally, be visited on the children, as well as the sins of the father. Good night, my rosebud. Good night, little woman. Pleasant slumbers! Happy dreams!'

Dickens, in this number, stresses the word 'cousin' in Ada's mouth, in reference to '*cousin* John'. It can mean, of course, simply that he is a kinsman, but we assume that Jarndyce may, in the past, have loved his other cousin, Ada's mother (as that other old bachelor, Boythorn, has a love somewhere in his past – whose identity we are still hopefully guessing at). Since he had never seen Ada before her recent arrival at Bleak House, how is it that he seems to have known her mother so well? The identity or character of Ada's father we never know (why was she left with only a small inheritance? Does she have siblings?) Dickens tantalises the reader throughout *Bleak House* with hints about missing, or half-glimpsed, parents.

What, gradually, are we learning about Esther's background?

After their return from visiting the incorrigibly restless Richard in London, John Jarndyce decides (belatedly, we may think – but suspense must be maintained), to inform Esther of what he knows of her 'history'. Neither of them can sleep and the exchange takes place in his 'growlery', or den, where he likes to contemplate the wretchedness of life, and confront it with his own inextinguishable optimism. What he actually knows of Esther's background is, he confesses, 'very little, next to nothing'. But it is an interesting next to nothing. Nine years ago he received a letter from a lady 'living in seclusion', saying that she wished to dispose of a little 'orphan girl then twelve years old'. This woman 'had blotted out all trace of her [the child's] existence' so that only she knew of her secret past. Clearly, too, she also wished to blot out any link, or connection of her own, with this girl. The reader will assume, of course, that the writer of this letter was a young Lady Dedlock, on the eve of her marriage into aristocracy and wanting to tie up some awkward loose ends. There is, however, no firm ground for this supposition. It could as well be Miss Barbary, disturbed at the prospect of a post-pubescent Esther living in her household, although how would Miss Barbary, in Windsor, know anything about John Jarndyce, whose philanthropy is invariably discreet?

John Jarndyce agreed to the appointment of Kenge as the confidential agent who, presumably, knows all the identities but remains professionally tight-lipped. For legal purposes (fictionally, we deduce), she – the mysterious woman – was to be Esther's 'aunt'. Presumably too, a sum of money was put in a trust fund to pay for Esther's boarding education until she should be able to join John Jarndyce as his housekeeper at Bleak House. John Jarndyce has, over the years, spied on Esther, assuring himself that she was a 'good girl'.

This explanation still leaves open the question of paternity. At this stage of the narrative, Esther routinely addresses John Jarndyce as 'Guardian' and the man who has been a 'Father to her'. During their highly charged conversation in the Growlery, the following exchange occurs:

> At the word Father, I saw his former trouble come into his face. He subdued it as before, and it was gone in an instant; but, it had been there, and it had come so swiftly upon my words that

> I felt as if they had given him a shock. I again inwardly re-
> peated, wondering, 'That I could readily understand. None
> that I could readily understand!' No, it was true. I did not
> understand it. Not for many and many a day.

This leaves open the possibility that John Jarndyce is, after all, her parent, or, alternatively, her hopeful husband. Tradition-ally in nineteenth-century novels, wards marry their guardi-ans – a distant peal of bells may be heard by the accustomed ear. Dickens slightly diverts this reader expectation by stress-ing the peripheral presence of Allan Woodcourt and the chime of different bells. Woodcourt is now practising what may be called 'telescopic medicine'. He cannot thrive in London, where his patients are mainly indigents like Miss Flite. He has taken ship to China, and to India, as a naval surgeon and is to be away a long time, but the East, in Dickens's world, always holds promise of future wealth. Who knows, he may return a nabob.

Esther's shame

One of the less lovely characters in the narrative is Allan Woodcourt's mother. Mrs Woodcourt is an arrant snob – a peculiarly obnoxious black beast in the Victorian menagerie. The term had been invented by Thackeray, in 1846, in his great anatomy of 'snobonomy', *The Snobs of England*. Although he does not use the term (Dickens had an awkwardly competitive relationship with Thackeray), the author of *Bleak House* is as much a snob-hater as the author of *Vanity Fair*. The principal offender, at this stage of the narrative, is Mrs Woodcourt, with her interminable boasts of the family connection with Morgan ap-Kerrig:

Mrs Woodcourt, after expatiating to us on the fame of her great kinsman, said that, no doubt, wherever her son Allan went, he would remember his pedigree, and would on no account form an alliance below it. She told him that there were many handsome English ladies in India who went out on speculation, and that there were some to be picked up with property; but, that neither charms nor wealth would suffice for the descendant from such a line, without birth: which must ever be the first consideration. She talked so much about birth that, for a moment, I half fancied, and with pain – but, what an idle fancy to suppose that she could think or care what mine was!

The Victorians were adept at circumlocution where things shameful (notably sex and excretion), were concerned. What Mrs Woodcourt insinuates, with this ostentatious display of pedigree, is her disinclination to have her wonderful (only) child ally himself with a bastard daughter of who knows who? It is not, given the prejudices of the time, an entirely unreasonable disinclination. The bastardy laws were oppressive in England and would continue to be oppressive for the best part of a century. The prejudice partly arose from the Anglo-Saxon principle of primogeniture – legitimacy was intimately tied in with the laws regulating property and its inheritance. Partly it was the evangelical revival, which made moral 'shame' an important instrument of national reform.

We learn in this number that while Ada and Richard are wards of court (entrusted to the care of John Jarndyce), Esther is his personal ward. Has he adopted her and made her legitimate? It seems, from later events, that he has not, although he could have done (it might have complicated any marriage plans).

Esther's birth is becoming the mystery at the heart of the plot. The mystery is both thinned and thickened on the trip the Bleak House company make to Boythorn in Lincolnshire. Here

Esther sees – for the first time consciously in her life – Lady Dedlock as she appears, grandly later than the rest of the congregation, to take up the family's private pew in church:

> Shall I ever forget the rapid beating at my heart, occasioned by the look I met, as I stood up! Shall I ever forget the manner in which those handsome proud eyes seemed to spring out of their languor, and to hold mine! It was only a moment before I cast mine down – released again, if I may say so – on my book; but, I knew the beautiful face quite well, in that short space of time.
>
> And, very strangely, there was something quickened within me, associated with the lonely days at my godmother's.

Did Lady Dedlock's face 'accidentally resemble my godmother's?' Esther goes on to later wonder. Dickens is clearly tipping his reader the wink and it will be an obtuse reader by now who has not rumbled the 'connexion' that Guppy made, all those chapters earlier, when he connected the face of Esther with the great portrait of Lady Dedlock at Chesney Wold.

But in *Bleak House*, uncovering one mystery merely generates another. Even if we have one entry on her (imaginary) birth certificate, what, precisely, were the *circumstances* of Esther's birth? Who, one wonders for the hundredth time, is her father? The storm scene, when Esther takes shelter with Lady Dedlock, raises other questions. Why has this great lady never taken the trouble to 'see' Esther – something that would have been easy enough. Storms in literature traditionally prefigure crisis. What, precisely, will that crisis be? Something more than a mere drenching in summer rain, we may be sure.

There are other recognitions, or half recognitions, in this powerful scene (made for TV, one would think). Lady Dedlock recognises John Jarndyce. It also emerges that John Jarndyce has petitioned Sir Leicester to 'advance' Richard's career. Why did he choose this patron (a man who is at daggers drawn with Jarndyce's best friend)? Typically, Sir Leicester does not have it 'in his power' to help Richard. Or, one suspects, in his inclination.

In their rather strained conversation during the storm Lady Dedlock talks of a time, many years ago, when she and John Jarndyce 'were in the habit of meeting'. More explicitly, and perplexingly, she adds: 'I think you knew my sister, when we were abroad together, better than you knew me'. Did John Jarndyce then, love the young woman to whom we were introduced as the puritanical Miss Barbary? Was Lady Dedlock also, in her youth, a Miss Barbary? And is Esther, so to speak, yet another? 'One would think that John Jarndyce, with such a degree of acquaintance with the Barbarys, must have a shrewd idea of what the story is. Or does he?

Having seen Esther, Lady Dedlock impulsively 'adopts' her orphan maid, Rosa, and peremptorily dismisses Hortense – a decision that turns out to be a big mistake.

Dickens's loathing of 'dilettantism'

One of Skimpole's sublimer flights of self-serving nonsense is that on slaves and slavery:

> 'Take an extreme case. Take the case of the Slaves on American plantations. I dare say they are worked hard, I dare say they don't altogether like it, I dare say theirs is an unpleasant experience on the whole; but, they people the landscape for me, they give it a poetry for me, and perhaps that is one of the pleasanter objects of their existence. I am very sensible of it, if it be, and I shouldn't wonder if it were!'

As *Martin Chuzzlewit* and *American Notes* make clear, Dickens loathed negro slavery, but had a Carlylean respect for what the Scottish sage called 'servantship'. Tony Weller, Mark Tapley, and (in *Bleak House*) the admirable Mrs Rouncewell are not slaves, but good servants, as in time Trooper George will be.

As Dickens's depiction of Skimpole indicates, he strongly disliked dilettantism. He saw it as intellectual dandyism – a refusal to be serious, or earnest. Dandyism, wholly disparaged in the post-Regency era, was rehabilitated (briefly, alas) in the 1890s around the meteoric rise of Oscar Wilde, only to crash with his trials and disgrace. Earnestness would rule once again. It is a nice mind game to speculate how a Dickens in his late eighties (not an impossible age), might have commented on Oscar. Skimpole would have adored him.

Why does Hortense stomp barefoot through the grass?

Vividly, out of fury at being publicly dismissed in favour of Rosa as Lady Dedlock's personal attendant, after the storm has passed (and Lady Dedlock has had her traumatic meeting with Esther), Hortense cools her fury in an odd way:

> without the least discomposure of countenance, [she] slipped off her shoes, left them on the ground, and walked deliberately in the same direction [as her mistress's coach], through the wettest of the grass.

What, one may wonder, does this dramatic, but enigmatic act, signify? Clearly that Hortense is a very angry (ex-)servant. Taken in conjunction with her sinister, southern Frenchness, we may feel a vibration of sansculottism and physical violence to come. Later when she offers her services to Esther, Miss Summerson declines, thinking that Hortense resembles to her mind 'some woman from the streets of Paris in the reign of terror'. The woman hinted at in Esther's remark will, of course, emerge fully formed seven years later as Madame Defarge in *A Tale of Two Cities*.

Chadband's religion

Social historians have identified the most powerful ideological impulse sweeping through, and transforming, Victorian England as evangelicalism. It was this moral-religious revival that instilled standards of decency, respectability, and the fear of God in the lower and lower-middle classes. Dickens had reservations about the more strident evangelicalism – satire which he discharges satirically on the revivalist preacher, Chadband:

> Mr Chadband is a large yellow man, with a fat smile, and a general appearance of having a good deal of train oil in his system. Mrs Chadband is a stern, severe-looking, silent woman. Mr Chadband moves softly and cumbrously, not unlike a bear who has been taught to walk upright. He is very much embarrassed about the arms, as if they were inconvenient to him, and he wanted to grovel; is very much in a perspiration about the head; and never speaks without first putting up his great hand, as delivering a token to his hearers that he is going to edify them.
>
> 'My friends,' says Mr Chadband, 'peace be on this house! On the master thereof, on the mistress thereof, on the young maidens, and on the young men! My friends, why do I wish for peace? What is peace? Is it war? No. Is it strife? No. Is it lovely, and gentle, and beautiful, and pleasant, and serene, and joyful? Oh, yes! Therefore, my friends, I wish for peace, upon you and upon yours.'

(Train oil, incidentally, has nothing to do with railways. It is whale oil: Moby Dick is harpooned for the greater glory of the Rev. Chadband.)

Chadband's preaching style is that associated with the annual Exeter Hall revival rallies in London that whipped up the religious-moral temperature in England, and that Dickens specifically targeted in the centre of his monthly wrapper. Chadband's torrent of sermonising is hilariously funny. He is another of those newly-introduced characters thrown on the narrative fire to keep it blazing. But there are also, inevitably, 'connexions'. It emerges that Mrs Chadband was connected with Esther before she became Mrs Chadband. She is, we realise, the former Miss Rachael.

Plate 23. Mr Chadband 'Improving' a Tough Subject

Move on!

The sixth number ends with a tableau: sunset, St Pauls, and Jo being 'moved on':

And there he sits, munching and gnawing, and looking up at the great cross on the summit of St. Paul's Cathedral, glittering above a red-and-violet-tinted cloud of smoke. From the boy's face one might suppose that sacred emblem to be, in his eyes, the crowning confusion of the great, confused city – so golden, so high up, so far out of his reach. There he sits, the sun going down, the river running fast, the crowd flowing by him in two streams—everything moving on to some purpose and to one end – until he is stirred up and told to 'move on' too.

Dickens is here tilting at the vagrancy laws, specifically the Metropolitan Police Acts of 1829 and 1839 that enacted a Victorian version of zero tolerance. The hard-heartedness of the current vagrancy laws had long been one of his journalistic targets and he had attacked them in his magazine, *Household Words*. They nonetheless survived until the 1970s as the loathed 'SUS' laws (i.e. 'suspected of loitering with intent'). Some dragons not even Dickens could kill.

*

Instalment 7 (Chapters 20–22),

September 1852

Summary

At this point Dickens takes measures to thicken the novel's plot. It is still summer, the dead time of year in legal (and high society) London. Everyone who is anyone is either in the country or abroad. Guppy, his fidus Achates, young Smallweed, 'Chick', an apprentice clerk, and Tony Jobling, a clerk recently 'sacked' for dishonesty, get together for a convivial lunch at a 'Slap Bang'. Guppy is still scheming to find out as much as he can about Esther – for whom his heart, as he sentimentally informs his friends, aches. Partly to ease that ache he installs Jobling in Nemo's vacated scrivener's job at Krook's lodging house, in Nemo's former room. His precise motive will appear later. Weevle is another lodger in Krook's house. Apart from his (feeble) whiskers, Weevle's prize possessions are his collections of pin-ups from 'The Divinities of Albion or Galaxy Gallery of British Beauty', high in whose parade is the stunning Lady Dedlock.

In addition to these new characters, Dickens introduces, at chapter length, the Smallweed family. Through the Smallweeds, yet another man of mystery, Trooper George, appears on the scene. He has, he says, been a 'thundering bad son' (there is a clue here to his identity, for those readers with long memories). An ex-military man, George is deeply in debt to the ruthless Smallweeds who run a money-lending business. George, whose surname is never vouchsafed, runs a not very

135

successful 'shooting gallery' off Leicester Square. His assistant is a cripple, Phil Squod (firearms will figure later in the criminal subplot of *Bleak House*; among others, the sharp-eyed reader will note, French women have been to George's gallery to improve their marksmanship). It emerges that George was a comrade of a 'Captain Hawdon' who was also deeply indebted to the Smallweeds – for gambling debts, as we deduce. Hawdon will become a centre of interest over the next few numbers. Charley is in the Smallweeds' employ, as a 'slavey' or servant girl, remorselessly bullied by Mrs Smallweed.

Another major player is introduced in the person of Chief Inspector Bucket of Scotland Yard. With Bucket's entry *Bleak House* takes a turn into detective fiction. He has been privately hired by Tulkinghorn (perfectly legal at this date) to crack the Dedlock/Nemo mystery. Snagsby has picked up something from Jo about the unconvincing servant lady in a 'wale', and is duly summoned, and examined by the sleuth and his employer. They then go to Tom-all-Alone's and question Jo. The astute Bucket has Hortense, Lady Dedlock's servant, do a one-person identity parade and Jo confirms the likeness. Hortense, we know, has been dismissed, or has dismissed herself. Later she will offer to serve Esther – who prudently refuses the offer. The brickmaker and his family, looking for work, are also at Tom-all-Alone's. Disease is ravaging them, and the whole slum tenement. It emerges that Bucket also has a warrant against Gridley, the maddened man from Shropshire, for disturbing the peace and criminal menace.

*

The Dickensian menu

The seventh number opens with a jolly lunch between the three clerks: Guppy, Jobling, and Smallweed (William, Tony, and 'Chick'). They go to a dining house, a nearby 'Slap Bang' – so called because of the speed with which the victuals appear and must be paid for. The fare is very different from the pub lunch or virtuous *Prêt a Manger* found around High Holborn in AD 2005. Descriptions of 'guttling' are a Dickensian speciality – this is one of the more mouth-wateringly detailed.

The 'legal triumvirate' enter, passing a window display of fresh vegetables and poultry. Within, customers are reading newspapers (the taxes on knowledge, introduced to suppress sedition in the Napoleonic Wars, drove the price of newspapers sky high – hence their being offered for collective reading in public dining and drinking places). Guppy is a 'regular', and is greeted as such. A full-sized 'bread', or loaf, is put on the table, 'blotched' with beer and grease from earlier feasts. Their order is shouted down the 'speaking pipe' (a primitive internal phone system) to the kitchens below, and is promptly brought up by dumb waiter. Speed is of the essence (a half-hour break for lunch was normal). The young diners are served by Polly.

They order veal and ham pie, french beans and stuffing (cheaper than a 'cut' from the day's joint). They also order a side order of summer cabbage ('without slugs, Polly!'). Pies (using up scraps of meat) were relatively long lasting, as was cured meat like ham. The joint would be fresh that day, and pie or stew tomorrow. The food is promptly served in plates with tin covers over them. The diners wash down their gubbins with three pints of 'half and half' – mild and bitter beer. Jobling (we begin to understand how it was he came to be 'sacked'), downs his pint quickly and is soon on to the second. For dessert, they have three marrow puddings followed by three cheshires (small cheeses) and three 'small rums' – the 'apex' of the meal. 'Il fo manger', as Jobling says ('pronouncing that word as if he meant a necessary fixture in an English stable'). And manger they richly have. What does it cost? Smallweed (offspring of a money-lending family) reckons the total up:

> 'Four veals and hams is three, and four potatoes is three and four, and one summer cabbage is three and six, and three marrows is four and six, and six breads is five, and three Cheshires is five and three, and four half-pints of half-and-half is six and three, and four small rums is eight and three, and three Pollys is eight and six. Eight and six in half a sovereign, Polly, and eighteenpence out!'

They leave Polly a threepenny tip. Guppy pays. Since, as we know from his marriage offer to Esther, he earns a measly two pounds a week, he has blown a substantial amount of his cash. He blows another one and sixpence buying a bottle of 'Lord Chancellor's eighteenpenny' (gin) to sweeten Krook. Why?

For 'Smallweed' read 'cash nexus'

The Smallweeds are a family that live by one law only – what Carlyle called 'cash nexus'. They are moneylenders. Money is to them what meat and drink are to other human beings. If Weevle is a maggot in the world of fashion, they are lice on the locks of capitalism. Calculation (interspersed with domestic battery against the senile Mrs Smallweed) dictates their life, or, as Dickens puts it, these old pagans' God was 'Compound Interest'. Chick (Bartholomew, or 'Bart'), was educated at a charity school (not because his family could not pay for his education, but they saw a better use for the money). He and his twin sister, Judith, are like two 'old monkeys'. They have never, in the whole of their childhood, been told a fairy story, or heard a nursery rhyme (Dickens will develop this theme with the 'people mutht be amuthed' narrative in *Hard Times*). Mr George (Trooper George, as we will know him) has fallen into their money-lending clutches. Bad luck him.

Plate 24. The Smallweed Family

Who is 'Captain Hawdon'?

When Trooper George drops by to renew his bill to the obnoxious Smallweeds and stops to take a pipe of tobacco (the only thing they ever 'give' him), conversation turns to Captain Hawdon, a former comrade of the Trooper's who reportedly owed the Smallweeds 'immense sums'. They have sought, unsuccessfully, to persuade George to track their debtor down, that they may dun him, but George stoutly refuses to betray a former comrade:

'I have been at his right hand many a day when he was charg-
ing upon ruin full-gallop. I was with him when he was sick and
well, rich and poor. I laid this hand upon him after he had run
through everything and broken down everything beneath him
– when he held a pistol to his head.'

The frequent references to Trooper George's bronzed face
suggest the two men served in India, perhaps fighting in the
Sikh Wars in the mid-1840s. Or perhaps (as it is later hinted) in
the West Indies – although there has been no recent fighting
there. Later Tulkinghorn (who, as usual, has done his research), says 'You served under Captain Hawdon at one time,
and were his attendant in illness, and rendered him many little
services, and were rather in his confidence, I am told.' George,
as Tulkinghorn indicates, was a sergeant, an NCO – not, like
Hawdon, a commissioned officer (whose commission would
have had to be bought). Hawdon evidently plunged into debt,
gambling, and came to the brink of suicide. As George tells the
seethingly frustrated Smallweeds:

'Don't lose your temper as well as your money,' says Mr.
George, calmly knocking the ashes out of his pipe. 'He was
drowned long before. I am convinced of it. He went over a
ship's side. Whether intentionally or accidentally, I don't know.
Perhaps your friend in the city does. Do you know what that
tune is, Mr. Smallweed?' he adds after breaking off to whistle
one, accompanied on the table with the empty pipe.
'Tune!' replied the old man. 'No. We never have tunes here.'

Trooper George is accompanying his remarks by humming
the Dead March from *Saul*. He may, of course, be lying. All's
fair in love, war, and wherever the Smallweeds are involved.
Or did Hawdon, like the hero of *Our Mutual Friend*, stage-man-
age his death by drowning, becoming one of the 'dead but not

dead' (as they were called in Victorian fiction)? Interestingly when he first meets Esther, George is convinced he has seen her somewhere before. It is, again, the likeness to her mother which strikes this chord. Clearly George knew something of the romantic complications of Hawdon's life. But what were they?

Enter the detective

Literary historians argue about the origins of the detective (or crime) novel in English. Poe has a strong claim, with Auguste Dupin and the *Murders in the Rue Morgue* (1843). So does *Bleak House* have a claim, with Chief Inspector Bucket. Dickens based Bucket on the 'thief taker', Inspector Charles Field, whom he had observed and written articles about a couple of years earlier. The modern detective that we know only too well was at this point a recent innovation. At this period, detectives could be hired by private individuals as 'confidential agents' ('private eyes', as we call them). Bucket is Tulkinghorn's PI. Much of the mystique about the detective craft derived from the memoirs of the French Sûrêté agent, E. F. Vidocq, whose memoirs were a bestseller. Like Vidocq (and, further down the line, Sherlock Holmes), Bucket is a master of disguise. To apprehend Gridley (a corpse, alas), he disguises himself as a benign old doctor. He has a whole army of agents posted around the streets, in plain clothes.

One of the features of the detective novel is that it creates detective readers. Details, apparently unimportant, are, on later recollection, 'motivated'. Take, for instance, the following passage about George's shooting gallery, which he describes to Esther (George has come to give Richard some broadsword exercises). He teaches marksmanship, he says. To what kind of person? John Jarndyce asks:

> 'All sorts, sir. Natives and foreigners. From gentlemen to 'prentices. I have had French women come, before now, and show themselves dabs at pistol-shooting. Mad people out of number, of course – but they go everywhere, where the doors stand open.'
>
> 'People don't come with grudges, and schemes of finishing their practice with live targets, I hope?' said my guardian, smiling.
>
> 'Not much of that, sir, though that has happened. Mostly they come for skill – or idleness. Six of one, and half a dozen of the other'.

This narrative time bomb (if that is what it is), will not explode for many chapters more.

*

Instalment 8 (Chapters 23–25),

October 1852

Hortense offers her services to Esther, who politely declines to take on the passionate Frenchwoman as her maid (it is a mark of her rise in life, however, that she can even think of such a thing).

Richard is embarked on yet another change of career: as an army officer. A commission is duly purchased for him (by Jarndyce, we assume). He is trained in some rudimentary military exercises by Trooper George (another connexion). It emerges in this number (via the Smallweeds) that Richard has been borrowing money in expectation of his great Jarndyce expectations. He is on the slippery slope. John Jarndyce reluctantly, but authoritatively, and in his office as court-appointed guardian, breaks the engagement which has been contracted between Ada and Richard. Henceforth they are to be cousins, and nothing more.

Caddy, under Esther's beneficient influence, continues to make progress in domestic skills and virtues. She has accepted Prince's proposal of marriage. Esther, to bolster her *prutégée's* confidence, accompanies her to the meeting of the two sets of parents. Mr Turveydrop goodnaturedly accepts, on the selfish grounds that he will now have two young people to keep him in the Regency style to which he is accustomed. Mrs Jellyby indifferently acquiesces – she has already employed a boy to address and stuff envelopes so she needs Caddy no longer. So preoccupied is she with her affairs on the left bank of the Niger that she neglects to notice that her husband has been made bankrupt.

John Jarndyce, who is more and more pleased with his 'little woman', gives Esther, by way of a reward, her personal maid – not the fearsome Hortense, but Charley, whom he has evidently released from the servitude of the Smallweed household. John Jarndyce has also put Charley's younger siblings, Tom and Emma, to school.

Gridley, who is dying of his mania, has taken refuge with Trooper George. His last wish is to see that other Jarndyce maniac, Miss Flite. He is being pursued by the remorseless (but not unsympathetic) Bucket, who has an arrest warrant from Tulkinghorn. The detective gains entrance to the shooting gallery by disguising himself as a physician. Too late. Gridley has only minutes to live. Esther meets Miss Rachael again, now as Mrs Chadband, who is elaborately courteous to the girl she once abused. Esther, we apprehend, is coming up in the world.

The number ends with Chadband in full sermonising flight at the Snagsbys. Jo is unimpressed. He still 'don't know nothink'.

*

'This weaving and spinning age'

Dickens frequently spices his narrative with contemporary newspaper references. This is October 1852. In his gracious consent to Prince marrying Caddy (on condition that he keeps earning to support his drone of a parent), Turveydrop grandiloquently wonders how he and his kind may 'linger in this weaving and spinning age'. The remark would have struck a chord in the contemporary reader. The biggest, longest, and best-covered trade union strike in English history was about to break out among the textile workers in Preston, Lancashire. It would supply the background to Dickens's next work, the social-problem novel *Hard Times* (1854).

Why does Jarndyce break the love birds' engagement?

John Jarndyce, against his habitual good nature, breaks off the engagement between Richard and Ada which, as court-appointed guardian (and they being under 21) he is legally empowered to do on the grounds of Richard's inability to settle in any of the courses of work John Jarndyce has opened to him and because, one may deduce, he has picked up the fact that Richard has been borrowing on the strength of his 'expectations'. It is one of the few occasions in the narrative when this sugar-daddy to all acts with firmness. From this hour, as Esther notes, Richard 'never was as free and open with Mr Jarndyce as he had been before'. Was there, perhaps, an unconscious sexual jealousy at work? At this stage, Richard is by no means a lost cause (no more than Pip, for example, in *Great Expectations*, in the period before Magwitch's return).

*

Instalment 9 (Chapters 26–29), November 1852

Summary

It is now winter in the narrative, as it was in the serial issue. A year has passed. We learn more of George's background (he was born in the country) and of Phil Squod's (he is a living anthology of industrial injuries). George is summoned to Tulkinghorn's chambers by Smallweed, who knows of the Trooper's Hawdon connection. A sample of Hawdon's writing is wanted so that Tulkinghorn may compare it with that script which so alarmed Lady Dedlock, a year ago. The Smallweeds also have their motive. Hawdon died, or disappeared, owing them money. It is suspected that George has such a sample (as indeed he does), but will he part with it? Tulkinghorn more and more suspects a connection with Lady Dedlock and is on her scent (as are Guppy and even, in her unsinister way, Esther). George, out of loyalty, refuses to hand over what is demanded from him. Threats are made against him.

Richard, we learn, is falling ever more into the rapacious grip of the Smallweeds, who see him as rich prey for their loan sharking. We also learn that George has secured his debt with the signature of another honourably discharged soldier, the ultra-military Matthew Bagnet (whose catchphrase is 'Discipline must be maintained'). Bagnet now earns his living as a theatrical musician and resides with his family (the children all named after military stations) around the Elephant and Castle.

Sir Leicester's noble equanimity is disturbed by a visit from the 'Ironmaster', the son of his housekeeper, Mrs Rouncewell who has made his fortune in the industrial north (and is going into politics – on the opposite side from Sir Leicester). The Ironmaster's son, Watt (named after the inventor of steam power), has conceived a romantic attraction to Lady Dedlock's new maid and *protégée*, Rosa. As a radical, the Ironmaster has no desire to have his future daughter-in-law attached to Chesney Wold (although he is happy that his mother remain there). Sir Leicester is mightily affronted. A standoff develops between these representatives of Old and New England. The Watt-Rosa engagement is, it seems, broken (it is clear on which side Dickens's sympathies lie, although he was to create a less friendly depiction of the Northern industrial magnate with Bounderby, in his next novel).

Guppy calls on Lady Dedlock and intimates that he is in a position to secure certain letters in Krook's possession that will embarrass her. He has noted the resemblance between her face and Esther's, and he has (via the Snagsbys), made the acquaintance of Mrs Chadband, née Rachael. He has for some time worked out that Miss Summerson is, in fact, Miss Hawdon. That night, at midnight, he will come into possession of Krook's letters via Jobling, whom he has, schemingly, inserted into the old illiterate's lodging house. When that packet changes hands, Lady Dedlock's secret will be William Guppy's. When Guppy leaves, Lady Dedlock's frigid composure dissolves into wild lamentation.

Among the new characters, along with the Ironmaster, introduced in this number, is the withered sprig of aristocracy, Volumnia Dedlock, Sir Leicester's cousin.

*

What is the significance of Phil Squod, in the great scheme of things?

Plate 25. Visitors to the Shooting Gallery – Phil Squod
cleans the guns at the shooting gallery

On the face of it, Phil is a Dickensian grotesque – a cripple, one of the novel's many sideshows (in his case, a freak show). But historically speaking, it is the industrial revolution that has crippled him. Phil Squod is another elephant man deformed by 'progress', George is sympathetic to his deformity:

> 'what with a dozen years in a dark forge, where the men was given to larking; and what with being scorched in a accident at a gasworks; and what with being blowed out of winder, case-filling at the firework business; I am ugly enough to be made a show on!'

· Such public displays of deformity ('raree' shows), were as much a feature of the Victorian cultural diet as bull-baiting was to the Elizabethan. Dickens (not entirely immune to the callousness of his age), created his own gallery of grotesques and freaks in his fiction with the loveable dwarf, Jennie Wren; the hateful dwarf, Quilp; the one-legged Wegg; and of course, Phil Squod.

What to do with the soldier when there is no war to fight?

There are emergent classes in *Bleak House*, such as the Ironmaster and his energetic son, Watt. There are decayed classes, such as the paralytic Dedlocks, the baronet's 'cousins', and the outlying Boodles and Coodles. There are vagrant classes, such as the brickmakers. And there are also the 'what shall we do with them?' classes. England had been at peace in Europe (the empire was something else), for an immensely long period. Military men like Captain Hawdon, Sergeant George and artilleryman Bagnet had no occupation. As Kipling observed, sarcastically, the image of Tommy Atkins changes drastically according to whether or not the war-bugles are blowing:

> I went into a public-'ouse to get a pint o' beer,
> The publican 'e up an' sez, 'We serve no red-coats here.'
> The girls be'ind the bar they laughed an' giggled fit to die,
> I outs into the street again an' to myself sez I:
> *O it's Tommy this, an' Tommy that, an' 'Tommy, go away';*
> *But it's 'Thank you, Mister Atkins', when the band begins to play,*
> *The band begins to play, my boys, the band begins to play,*
> *O it's 'Thank you, Mister Atkins', when the band begins to play.*

The Atkinses in *Bleak House* are all adrift. Hawdon has become an indigent clerk (less efficient, clearly, than the unimpressive Jobling), and a drug addict. George runs a money-devouring shooting gallery and will soon find himself in the bankruptcy courts. Bagnet scrapes by as an oboist in a theatre specialising in patriotic shows. All this would change, a year after *Bleak House*, with the Crimea and the emergence of the kind of 'muscular' military heroes popularised most successfully by Charles Kingsley (Amyas Leigh, Hereward the Wake, for example). Dickens's novel catches poor Tommy at a low ebb.

Parent power

Plate 26. The Ironmaster

When the Ironmaster comes down to Chesney Wold to declare the conditions under which he will permit Rosa to make an alliance with him (a member of the new, working aristocracy), he lays down the law with the severity of an Old Testament patriarch:

'"Therefore I shall have this girl educated for two years," – or, it may be – "I shall place this girl at the same school with your sisters for such a time, during which you will give me your word and honour to see her only so often. If, at the expiration of that time, when she has so far profited by her advantages as that you may be upon a fair equality, you are both in the same mind, I will do my part to make you happy." I know of several cases such as I describe, my Lady, and I think they indicate to me my own course now.'

At this display of radical independence (not to say impertinence), 'Sir Leicester's magnificence explodes. Calmly, but terribly'. The modern reader might also respond explosively at the refusal to allow twenty-something Rosa and Watt any independence in their life choices. What right has a father to dictate thus? And not just the Ironmaster, but father-figure John Jarndyce, who takes it on himself to break up the Richard–Ada engagement. Or Turveydrop, who has it in his power to forbid his son Prince to marry the woman he loves. One of the social facts of Victorian life which it is hard for the modern viewer/reader to come to terms with is the unquestioned dictatorial power of the parental class (certainly unquestioned by Charles Dickens, who was very much the authoritarian paterfamilias to his brood). The reasons were wholly economic. It took infinitely longer to accumulate the financial wherewithal to marry. Hence that uniquely Victorian institution, the long engagement.

Tennyson, for example, was obliged to wait many long years to marry the woman he loved. Within this novel, Esther and Allan must wait. Unsurprisingly, given this imbalance of power, there are relatively few good fathers to be found in Victorian fiction.

What *were* the circumstances of Esther's birth?

To this point, the viewer/reader will have constructed various plausible hypotheses. There may have been a marriage between Hawdon and Miss Barbary (the younger), and a child born to them. The marriage must have broken up and the child would have been taken, at the mother's expense and with her full knowledge, to lodge with her (the child's) aunt, Miss Barbary. Alternatively, there might have been no such marriage. Esther is in fact illegitimate, and her mother took care to keep her out of the way, forwarding money for that purpose to her sister. At the end of Chapter 29, however, in a passionate outburst after Guppy (having indicated his blackmailing scheme) has left, Lady Dedlock cries out:

> 'O my child, my child! Not dead in the first hours of her life, as my cruel sister told me, but sternly nurtured by her, after she had renounced me and my name! O my child, O my child!'

It is an awkwardly melodramatic outburst stylistically – more in keeping with Mrs Henry Wood and *East Lynne* ('Dead! Dead! and never called me mother!') than *Bleak House*, but it offers a new and, for most viewers / readers, somewhat unpredicted key to the novel's central mystery. This revelation may signal a slight loss of nerve, on Dickens's part – an inability to go through with some previous plot design. The likelihood that Lady Dedlock would have had a child living, brought up to adulthood by her sister (the only surviving member of her family), and not know about it, seems unlikely. Who was it, one wonders, who wrote to John Jarndyce claiming support for the twelve-year-old Esther? Miss Barbary seems an unlikely candidate. Did the father of the child (Hawdon) also never know of Esther's survival? What possible motive can Miss Barbary have had for this (criminal) deception?

*

Instalment 10 (Chapters 30–32),

December 1852

Summary

Mrs Woodcourt comes to Bleak House and continues her campaign of discouragement against Esther, by tedious reference to Allan's noble pedigree. Esther, she insists, must have no 'mistaken notions'. Interestingly, Mrs Woodcourt hints that Esther will marry John Jarndyce. After Mrs Woodcourt's departure, Caddy Jellyby visits. She is to be married in a month and Esther takes charge of the proceedings, choosing the dress, arranging the reception and smoothing things over with the wholly useless parents, Mrs Jellyby and Mr Turveydrop. Mr Jellyby is still in a condition of melancholy madness, bankrupt and wordless. His one statement in the novel is (to Caddy) 'Never have a Mission, my dear child'. The wedding, thanks to Esther, is not a disaster.

Charley informs Esther that the brickmaker's family have returned from the 'tramp' and are again in the St Albans area. There is serious sickness in the family. Esther goes off to visit and bring them medicine. En route they come across Jo, who is also fever-stricken and delirious – obsessed with the lady who gave him the sovereign. He has been 'moved on' and 'hunted down'. Esther takes the sick boy back to Bleak House. John Jarndyce regards the boy charitably. Skimpole, by contrast, takes one look and observes: 'You had better turn him out' (and, we will discover, eventually takes his own selfish measures in that direction). There is only room for one cuckoo in the Jarndyce nest. Jo, mysteriously, disappears from Bleak House where he was being looked after. Why? He has, however, left something behind him. Smallpox. Charley is the first to fall victim. Then Esther succumbs. She is first blinded (temporarily) then disfigured (permanently) with the disease (Dickens, cunningly, leaves a month's suspense before the reader will know whether or not Esther will lose her sight forever).

The scene switches to Krook's lodging house. At midnight, the packet of letters which will destroy Lady Dedlock is to be handed over. Guppy and Weevle foregather with Tony in Nemo's old room (where Jobling now lodges). They are strangely uneasy. On going down to the landlord's room, Tony discovers that the old drunkard has exploded. 'Spontaneous Combustion', believe it or not (some did, some didn't).

*

Who will Esther marry?

In his notes for this section of the novel, Dickens was careful to remind himself that Esther's love dilemma must be kept in the foreground of the novel ('Esther's love must be kept in view, to make the coming trial the greater and the victory the more meritorious'). The reader will be in two minds about which of the eligibles this pearl among women should, ideally, hitch up with. The penurious but worthy surgeon, or the rich philanthropist who has taken such care of her. That the uncertainty should be in the reader's mind is confirmed by Dickens having Mrs Woodcourt observe (while warning Esther off Allan):

> 'you will marry some one very rich and very worthy, much older – five and twenty years, perhaps – than yourself. And you will be an excellent wife, and much beloved, and very happy.'

Mrs Woodcourt, in her shrewd way, has noticed that John Jarndyce has given 'Dame Durden', the 'mistress of the keys' all the privileges of marriage bar one: the double bed.

Feminism: the Dickensian counter-revolution continues

Plate 27. 'Never have a mission, my dear child.'
– Mr Jellyby advises Caddy

The melancholy, mad Mr Jellyby has but one piece of advice for his daughter, Caddy, as she embarks on marriage with Prince: 'Never have a Mission, my dear child'. That is, never have an activity outside the home – which is woman's natural sphere. Dickens stresses the point with the introduction of Miss Wisk (soon to be the partner of Mr Quale – the unlovely philanthropic suitor Mrs Jellyby initially planned for her daughter). Miss Wisk incarnates everything Dickens despises in aspirant womanhood (the 'shrieking sisterhood' as they would be called, ten years later):

> Miss Wisk's mission, my guardian said, was to show the world that woman's mission was man's mission; and that the only

genuine mission, of both man and woman was to be always moving declaratory resolutions about things in general at public meetings.

These public meetings, ostensibly for charitable purposes, were (principally in London and Boston, USA) the germ of what would become the women's movement. Five years later, its pressure would have its first success with the 1857 'Matrimonial Causes' (i.e. divorce) Act and a series of reforms enabling women, like men, to be property holders. At the end of the line was the holy grail – the vote. On the evidence of *Bleak House*, over Dickens's dead body. Which, coming as it did in 1917, it indeed was.

Esther's educational system: or non-system

Esther – the true feminist – teaches Caddy (who, having served as her mother's secretary, is very literate), to sew and Charley (who is nimble with her needle), to write. Neither is very successful at what does not come naturally to them, but this practical (unsystematic) mode of education works. Dickens will develop his educational theories at greater length in *Great Expectations* (specifically in the person of the self-taught village teacher, Biddy). The essence of the Dickensian philosophy is practicality. Snagsby's half crown is worth much more than Chadband's gusts of evangelical wind.

Jo and pox

Skimpole's advice to cast Jo out from Bleak House is cruel, but in one aspect sensible. Jo brings with him that dreaded visitor, smallpox. Charley is the first to fall ill, then Esther (who nursed Charley, reversing their roles) succumbs.

Plate 28. Nurse and patient – Ada nurses Charley
through smallpox

Esther is first struck blind by the disease (which, oddly, Dickens never names), then permanently 'pocked'. Smallpox, as dreaded as the other pox, has in the twenty-first century, been eradicated worldwide. It was common, and occasionally epidemic, in the nineteenth century. Oddly, none of the inhabitants of Bleak House seem to have been inoculated. Dickens was a shrewd observer of disease, but his medical theory was limited. As *Bleak House* indicates, he believed in the miasmic theory of infection, believing that foul air engendered disease.

> It is a close night, though the damp cold is searching too, and there is a laggard mist a little way up in the air. It is a fine steaming night to turn the slaughter-houses, the unwholesome trades, the sewerage, bad water, and burial-grounds to account, and give the registrar of deaths some extra business. It may be something in the air – there is plenty in it.

In fact, the disease vectors were often quite other as, with his pioneering work on waterborne disease, Dr John Snow was currently demonstrating.

Spontaneous combustion

The tenth number has two of what Victorian serialists would call 'tremendous scenes', and modern Hollywood would call 'money shots'. Esther being struck blind by smallpox is one. The other is the spontaneous combustion of Krook. The actual description of the syrupy and filthy remains of the exploded Krook is one of the most charged moments in Dickensian writing. The author bursts off the page to launch his *j'accuse* at the rulers of England (including even the monarch – note the reference to 'Your Highness'):

> Here is a small burnt patch of flooring; here is the tinder from a little bundle of burnt paper, but not so light as usual, seeming to be steeped in something; and here is – is it the cinder of a small charred and broken log of wood sprinkled with white ashes, or is it coal? O Horror, he IS here! and this, from which we run away, striking out the light and overturning one another into the street, is all that represents him.
>
> Help, help, help! come into this house for Heaven's sake!
>
> Plenty will come in, but none can help. The Lord Chancellor of that Court, true to his title in his last act, has died the death of all Lord Chancellors in all Courts, and of all authorities in all places under all names soever, where false pretences are made, and where injustice is done. Call the death by any name Your Highness will, attribute it to whom you will, or say it might have been prevented how you will, it is the same death eternally – inborn, inbred, engendered in the corrupted humours of the vicious body itself, and that only – Spontaneous Combustion, and none other of all the deaths that can be died.

Famously, the spontaneous combustion episode landed Dickens in furious controversy. The term was routinely applied to the burning down of hayricks which, if damp, can combust from the chemical breakdown of organic components in the hay (of course, they were also fired by criminals and political dissidents). But human beings, even human beings as sodden as Krook, are not hayricks. Reviewing the novel as it was appearing serially, G. H. Lewes (George Eliot's consort) made the observation that the explosion of Krook as a result of overindulgence in gin was scientifically nonsensical – culpably so. A violent exchange of polemics between the two men of letters – both arguing their corners by reference to 'science' ensued (of which, to be honest, Lewes was the better informed). The dispute rumbled on for months, with Dickens receiving distinctly the worst of it.

With hindsight (and a hundred and fifty years of literary criticism), the modern reader/viewer can easily resolve the controversy. With 'spontaneous combustion' Dickens was creating a metaphor for the socially explosive consequences of evil systems such as British law. But Dickens always regarded himself as a realist – not a poet. Anything which seemed to question the literal 'truth' of his writing was anathema to him. Although, at the time, Lewes won game, set and match, Dickens turned out to be right in a way. In America, in the 1980s, authorities were baffled by an increasing number of cases in which bodies were found, reduced to small piles of ash, with no sign of any foul play or any other plausible explanation. 'Spontaneous Combustion' was suspected. Forensic research revealed that if someone – usually paralytic drunk and smoking – fell into comatose sleep the blanket could smoulder and the effect of heat on the sleeper would release sufficient body fat to produce a 'candlewick effect'. Over a period of hours, as with a candle, this process could reduce a human body to nothing more than a heap of ash. Somewhere the shade of Dickens must have chortled.

Mr Dickens steps forward

Plate 29. The Appointed Time – Guppy discovers the spontaneously combusted remains of Krook

Under the intense pressure of the Spontaneous Combustion scene – one of the greatest scenes in the Dickensian *oeuvre* – something strange happens in terms of narrative decorum. At the end of the passage we are not reading a novel at all. Mr Dickens, social reformer, is talking to us directly across the novel (see above). How to handle this? Dickens is telling us that, in the last analysis, there are more important things than fiction. The novel dissolves, leaving a scandal that must be dealt with.

As it happens, Andrew Davies likes direct address to the camera – he too likes to dissolve the aesthetic distances that

separate performer from spectator. This however, is dangerous. When the novel restarts, we have to go back to our
original positions and Dickens had a month for the Spontaneous Combustion dust (or syrup, in Krook's case) to settle.
Davies only has a couple of days.

*

Instalment 11 (Chapters 33–35),

January 1853

Summary

This number opens with a second Coroner's Inquest at the Sol's Arms, with all the same macabre, fun-of-the-fair entertainment that we saw at the last inquest, and compered, as before, by the pub's landlord, Mr James George Bogsby. Once again Mr Swills does his music hall turn: this time with even grislier raw material for his comedy. Mr Snagsby and others give evidence as to the demise of Krook. The 'legal triumvirate' (who are becoming increasingly uncomradely), keep their motives for having foregathered at midnight on the night Krook died to themselves. It emerges, to everyone's surprise, that the rag and bottle merchant was the brother of Mrs Smallweed.

The web connecting the dramatis personae becomes ever more intricate. The old villain died intestate and his heirs begin to rummage through his papers (the incriminating evidence against Lady Dedlock is, however, lost). Krook is found to have died of Spontaneous Combustion. He exploded, in consequence of drinking raw gin. Lady Dedlock has a final interview with a discomfited Guppy (who will now never have the means to blackmail Esther's mother with the evidence of her maternity).

The Smallweeds, who figure centrally in this portion of the narrative, threaten to sell up Trooper George unless he acquiesces with Tulkinghorn's demand for a sample of Hawdon's handwriting. Since George has induced Matthew Bagnet to countersign his 'bill' with the Smallweeds, and neither of the signatories are able to raise the £94.7s.4d owed the stony-hearted Joshua (and his mythical accomplice in the city), the military oboist and his family will be rendered bankrupt and destitute. With much heartache, George finally surrenders a sample of Nemo's handwriting to his other hard-hearted persecutor, Tulkinghorn, and the selling up of the Bagnet household is averted.

Esther, meanwhile, is recovering slowly from the smallpox. Charley, in her kindness to her beloved mistress, has removed all looking glasses from the convalescent's rooms, but Esther demands to see the damage the disease has wrought. She takes her 'disfigurement' stoically, although it means the end of any hope of marriage with Allan Woodcourt. A 'conspiracy' is mobilised to make her happy.

Miss Flite calls to visit. We learn about her tragic family background and the monstrous incompetence of Chancery that has ruined the poor little lady and driven her to her current state of ornithological madness. She communicates some intelligence about the brickmaker's family, specifically Jenny, who reveres Esther. A lady (called Dedlock, of course) has called at the brickmakers' hovel, asking about Esther and taking, as a memento, a handkerchief that Miss Summerson had left there. Miss Flite, also utters some prophetic warning about Richard's downward path and informs Esther that Allan was shipwrecked and performed heroically. Boythorn offers Esther hospitality at Chesney Wold, so she may convalesce in the pure country air.

The Smallweeds: loan sharks or the
small man's banker?

Dickens, with the full blast of his awesome rhetoric, ensures that the reader hates the Smallweed family – the incarnation of Carlyle's loathed 'cash nexus'. There is, we are shown, a kernel of pure sadism at their core, as when, dropping all his customary smarm, Joshua Smallweed erupts at George who has asked what the letter, threatening to sell him up, 'means':

> Mr Smallweed, purposely balking himself in an aim at the trooper's head, throws the pipe on the ground and breaks it to pieces.
>
> 'That's what it means, my dear friend. I'll smash you. I'll crumble you. I'll powder you. Go to the devil!'
>
> The two friends rise and look at one another. Mr Bagnet's gravity has now attained its profoundest point.
>
> 'Go to the devil!' repeats the old man. 'I'll have no more of your pipe-smokings and swaggerings. What? You're an independent dragoon, too! Go to my lawyer (you remember where; you have been there before), and show your independence now, will you? Come, my dear friend, there's a chance for you. Open the street door, Judy; put these blusterers out! Call in help if they don't go. Put 'em out!'

The reader/viewer quivers with righteous rage, just as Dickens and Andrew Davies intend they should. 'Exterminate the brutes!' But on more mature reflection, are these loathsome specimens of unbridled capitalism, these monsters of usury, not, in their odious way, performing a valuable social function? Trooper George can hardly go to a bank to get a loan to finance the setting-up of his shooting gallery in the West End. He may have left the service with a small 'bounty', but it would have been too little to set up in business. No bank (certainly not Dickens's bank, Coutts), would support an ex-sergeant who has apparently joined the army with the same motive that inspired criminals to join the Foreign Legion – to bury his past. The Smallweeds, with the necessary guarantees (a co-signature of the Bagnets' on the bill), advance him money at interest. He can pay off the debt ('retire the bill') whenever he wishes. If he thrives he may make his way in the world – thanks to the Smallweed start-up loan.

One of the reasons that there is so much need for 'Charity' in *Bleak House* (Snagsby's half crowns, John Jarndyce's innumerable donations, subscriptions, handouts and unofficial pensions), is the fact that the mass of the British people have no access to credit. Take, for example, the Flite history, which we learn about in this number for the first time:

> 'Let me see,' said she. 'I'll tell you my own case. Before they ever drew me – before I had ever seen them – what was it I used to do? Tambourine playing? No. Tambour work. I and my sister worked at tambour work. Our father and our brother had a builder's business. We all lived together. Ve-ry respectably, my dear! First, our father was drawn – slowly. Home was drawn with him. In a few years, he was a fierce, sour, angry bankrupt without a kind word or a kind look for any one. He had been so different, Fitz-Jarndyce. He was drawn to a debtor's prison. There he died. Then our brother was drawn – swiftly – to drunkenness. And rags. And death. Then my sister was drawn. Hush! Never ask to what! Then I was ill, and in misery; and heard, as I had often heard before, that this was all the work of Chancery. When I got better, I went to look at the Monster. And then I found out how it was, and I was drawn to stay there.'

A little outside investment could have saved the genteelly hard-working Flites. Dickens is blazing away with his biggest guns, one feels, but he is missing some important targets. It is financial credit and trust rather than charity that is most needed. Dickens resorts instead to a sub-Christian optimism about the essential goodness of the monied classes (e.g. John Jarndyce), in undertaking a benevolent redistribution of wealth. Jarndyce is a one-man Victorian Oxfam, but even his pathological open-handedness cannot fund Victorian society's need for capital investment at all levels – from Isambard Kingdom Brunel to Trooper George.

What did Trooper George do in his youth that turned his mother's hair white?

Mrs Rouncewell, the doughty housekeeper, has two sons: the Ironmaster and the Trooper. Their relationship is that of Hogarth's Idle and Industrious Apprentice. The Ironmaster turned to industry and has made his fortune in the industrial north. He is now a Captain of Industry – one of Carlyle's new working aristocracy. He and his peers are making Britain the workshop of the world. George ran away to the army (helping make Britain master of the globe), and has not been heard from by his family since. There is a poignant moment with the Bagnet family when he looks at 'Woolwich' and says:

> 'The time will come, my boy,' pursues the trooper, 'when this hair of your mother's will be grey, and this forehead all crossed and re-crossed with wrinkles – and a fine old lady she'll be then. Take care, while you are young, that you can think in those days, "I never whitened a hair of her dear head, I never marked a sorrowful line in her face!" For of all the many things that you can think of when you are a man, you had better have that by you, Woolwich!'

What naughtiness, one wonders, can George have perpetrated in his youth? It evidently goes beyond adolescent, heel-kicking wildness. He does not, as far as we know, drink. He does not, like Nemo, dose himself with opium. He does not gamble. He has not, apparently, seduced and abandoned any young maidens. If there were bastards at Chesney Wold, we would presumably know about them. He is not, apparently, smitten with any particular remorse for any particular act. He has even, we gather (from oblique references to his comradeship with Hawdon) been a gallant solider and was honorably discharged from the service. Nevertheless he has been cut off entirely from his family. Interestingly the one thing he never thinks about when the Smallweeds drive him to the wall, is applying to his rich brother, for whom ninety-four pounds would be small change.

Every time George appears, the question of what he did in the past, hovers over his grizzled pate. When she finally appears in Chapter 55, Mrs Rouncewell sheds little light on the matter: 'He had a bold spirit, and he ran a little wild, and went for a soldier.' Her explanation for his lack of contact is that he was ashamed of having missed out on a commissioned rank, which seems an unlikely explanation for the complete severance of his relationship with her. Some fog in this novel never clears.

Dickens and the new aristocracy project

When Miss Flite, as part of the general conspiracy to cheer Esther up, tells her about Allan's heroism at sea ('An awful scene. Death in all shapes ... There, and through it all, my dear physician was a hero') the word Hero resonates – or, at least, it would with the Victorian reader. The echo thrown back would be 'Carlyle', who believed, as he outlined in his extraordinarily influential lectures on 'Heroes' (1841), that English society should be organised, hierarchically, around 'hero worship' – reverence, that is, for the noblest aspects of human behaviour.

Carlyle also argued for a 'new aristocracy' – as radical a project in 1847 as New Labour was in 1997. Britain's established peerage, baronetage, and nobility, were as ossified and useless as those of France in 1780. They served no function, offering no inspiration as role models to their inferiors. What kind of society is it that has, as its role model, Sir Leicester Dedlock? This was a society paralysed by protocol; suffocated by etiquette and propriety. Could Dedlock – even before the gout disabled him – 'rescue' anyone in the event of emergency or catastrophe, as Allan Woodcourt does? No, Sir Leicester would require his servants to do such tasks for him. Why won't Allan get a title? Miss Flite innocently asks. Esther (clearly speaking with Dickens's voice and Carlyle's sentiments) responds:

> I said it was not the custom in England to confer titles on men distinguished by peaceful services, however good and great; unless occasionally, when they consisted of the accumulation of some very large amount of money.
>
> 'Why, good gracious,' said Miss Flite, 'how can you say that? Surely you know, my dear, that all the greatest ornaments of England, in knowledge, imagination, active humanity, and improvement of every sort, are added to its nobility! Look round you, my dear, and consider, you must be rambling a little now, I think, if you don't know that this is the great reason why titles will always last in the land!'
>
> I am afraid she believed what she said; for there were moments when she was very mad indeed.

How much better society would be, however, were it headed by the likes of Allan Woodcourt. If nothing else, Dickens would be staunchly behind the Blairite initiative on reform of the Lords and some un-Blairite reform of the Honours List.

*

Instalment 12 (Chapters 36–38),
February 1853

Summary

Esther goes with the faithful Charley to recuperate in Lincoln-shire. It will not, alas, be an entirely quiet few weeks for our heroine (as she now is). In the country Esther makes herself useful to, and loved by, the villagers (illiterate peasants, for the main part). As always, she is quick to instruct and help – her needle and pen always at the ready. On one occasion, she is struck by a village wedding, which causes a pang around her heart. More ominously she goes into that part of the wood where there is the Ghost's Walk.

A ghost will indeed soon walk through her life. It is here that she meets Lady Dedlock. She asks that Charley walk some way ahead, out of earshot, and there is a passionate moment of recognition between mother and daughter. 'Oh my child, my child, I am your wicked and unhappy mother!', Lady Dedlock exclaims, disdaining to soften the blow. An explana-tion (not entirely satisfactory) is offered. Lady Dedlock, long before she bore that title, lived in ignorance of the survival of her child, even though the child was looked after, at someone else's expense, by Lady Dedlock's own sister. She only became aware of Esther's existence at the stormy meeting the previous summer at Chesney Wold.

They agree to keep apart from each other and kiss 'for the last time'. They also agree to keep 'their' secret. But is it safe? Esther says that John Jarndyce does not suspect, but they agree that he, alone, may be confided in. Lady Dedlock says that she believes that Tulkinghorn suspects. She gives Esther a letter, telling her the circumstances of her being 'laid aside as dead' at birth and her sister (unknowingly to the mother) taking charge of the disgraceful evidence of family shame – and subsequently declining into religious mania, we deduce, under the pressure of that shame.

A littler later Ada comes down to visit Esther. There is a mysterious night-time summons to the local pub, the Dedlock Arms. Who should be there but Richard (now wholly estranged from his erstwhile benefactor, John Jarndyce). Skimpole, disastrously, is now Richard's counsellor (and a leech on his flesh; for five pounds he has introduced him to that other leech, the lawyer Vholes). He is falling dangerously into debt. Although he is manifestly succumbing to the 'family curse', Esther still hopes against hope that the engagement with Ada (and friendly relations with her guardian), can be restored. Ada sends him a letter, imploring him to come to his senses, but her efforts are futile. Richard leaves Chesney Wold with Vholes, the latter looking like a bird of prey contemplating its victim.

Esther, more happily, returns to Bleak House, 'perfectly restored to health and strength'. One of her first visits is to Caddy Turveydrop (as the former Miss Jellyby now is), and Prince's dancing academy. Esther is becoming more assertive and positively rebuffs the unwanted civilities of Deportment Turveydrop, Prince's preposterous parent. There is a piece of business which Esther has to accomplish in London and she asks Caddy to accompany her. The piece of business is to visit Mr Guppy in his mother's house in Old Street. The young clerk is much discomfited, thinking that the disfigured Esther has come to force him to honour his offer of marriage, something which for two reasons he regrets having made; firstly because she is no longer beautiful, secondly because he no longer expects to get proof of her (monied) origins from Krook. Esther assures the young cad that she has no intention of keeping him to his word. Needless to say, she would never have married Guppy, but the scene confirms her acceptance of the fact that, marked as she is (by the shame of her birth as well as the smallpox), she will now never marry anyone.

*

What has the smallpox done to Esther, exactly?

Whereas Dickens could gloss over this problem on the printed page, the TV adaptation will have no such luxury. Dickens's illustrator, Hablôt K. Browne, was not commissioned to give any clear image of the pocked Esther (nor, given the limitations of engravings on steel, could he have done so with any precision). Esther habitually wears a veil at Chesney Wold, lifting it only, for example, to kiss Richard at the Dedlock Arms.

She is reconciled to her disfigurement: 'I had never been a beauty, and had never thought myself one; but I had been very different from this. It was all gone now.' But in what way 'gone'? Dickens and Thackeray were, although they rarely admitted it, rivals. In his concurrent novel, *Henry Esmond* (1852), Thackeray disfigures his heroine, Rachel Castlewood, with smallpox. In her case, as Thackeray put it, the effects of the disease were as if a fine painting in oils were 'smudged'. The complexion, that is, was coarsened. At a later point in the narrative Esther mentions 'scars' (presumably pockmarks). All things considered it is more likely her major loss was of that radiance of complexion which the nineteenth century called 'bloom'.

What is Esther's relationship to
John Jarndyce?

Esther's repetitive stress on the word 'Guardian' with reference to John Jarndyce, may lead the reader to wonder whether she has been legally adopted. The same issue arises with David Copperfield and Betsey Trotwood in Dickens's previous novel. As in *David Copperfield*, it seems that Esther's adoption is an informal, and not a binding, arrangement. It is clear that John Jarndyce has made a legal undertaking *vis-à-vis* Richard and Ada that is binding in law. They are wards of court and he is the trustee of the court, but this is not the case with Esther. She apparently appropriates the role of ward for herself and he is her guardian only because she calls him her guardian. There is an interesting moment, a little later in the narrative, when she ponders on what her situation would be were John Jarndyce to marry. In that event she would no longer be mistress of Bleak House and John Jarndyce would have no legal obligation towards her.

How should we react to Victorian 'O.T.T.'?

'One would need a heart of stone', said Oscar Wilde, 'not to laugh at the death of Little Nell'. Writing at the end of the century, Wilde was anticipating an essentially modern psychology – cool, collected and ironic. We, in general, do not weep. 'When a modern Englishman is overcome by emotion', said W. B. Yeats, 'he looks into the fire'. That was not the case with Victorian gentlemen. They would quite likely extinguish the fire with their lachrymosity.

It was even less the case with Victorian ladies. Women, nowadays, do not cultivate the art of 'fainting' at moments of stress – requiring the chafing of wrists, smelling salts, and the burning of feathers under the nose. Why did they faint? Tight corseting and poor diets have been suggested, but the most likely explanation was that women of the era executed a learned response – just as learned as our own tight lips and stoicism. This difference creates problems for us. How, for example, should the modern reader respond to Lady Dedlock's wild emotionalism on meeting Esther (who is also wildly emotional) in the Ghost's Walk:

> I looked at her; but I could not see her, I could not hear her, I could not draw my breath. The beating of my heart was so violent and wild, that I felt as if my life were breaking from me. But when she caught me to her breast, kissed me, wept over me, compassionated me, and called me back to myself; when she fell down on her knees and cried to me, 'O my child, my child,

Plate 30. Lady Dedlock in the Wood

I am your wicked and unhappy mother! O try to forgive me!' – when I saw her at my feet on the bare earth in her great agony of mind, I felt, through all my tumult of emotion, a burst of gratitude to the providence of God that I was so changed as that I never could disgrace her by any trace of likeness; as that nobody could ever now look at me, and look at her, and remotely think of any near tie between us.

The extremity of feeling and melodrama in the utterance (every word, practically, loaded with an exclamation mark), represents a challenge to the modern actor and director. Should it be hammed up on the grounds of 'when in Victorian fiction, do as the Victorians do'? Or should it somehow be 'translated' into our cooler, more disciplined style of response? Over to you, Andrew Davies.

*

Instalment 13 (Chapters 39–42),

March 1853

Summary

A year has passed both for the reader and for the personages of *Bleak House*. The twelfth number saw the entry of a new character who will, like a termite, burrow into the fabric of the narrative: the Attorney, Mr Vholes. Vholes, introduced to Richard Carstone by the indefatigably mischievous Skimpole, inflames the young man's obsession with 'the unmentionable' – Jarndyce versus Jarndyce. Collaterally, he inflames Carstone's increasingly irrational vendetta against John Jarndyce. It is now Carstone versus Jarndyce. The cadaverous Vholes ('a very respectable man') has daughters, an aged parent, and a disordered digestion. He never eats (unless his worm-like consumption of Richard's substance be nourishment to him). He is the embodiment of the universal rule that 'The one great principle of the English Law is to make business for itself'. He battens on Richard, whose army career is not going well, all the more sinister in that he is not personally malignant, but merely the perfect embodiment of the parasitism of the English legal system.

Young Smallweed has given up his position with Kenge and devotes himself now to the family business (the Smallweeds are still rummaging through the mounds of Krook's filthy jumble in the hopes of finding valuable documents). Tulkinghorn has an encounter with Guppy in which he makes clear that he is aware of Guppy's knowledge of Lady Ded-lock's secret.

A general election is imminent and has thrown torpid Chesney Wold into unwonted excitement. Whig Coodle is contesting the election with Tory Sir Thomas Doodle (Sir Leicester's candidate, needless to say). Among the company gathered for the election at Chesney Wold is Volumnia Dedlock, a withered sprig of the family and a pensioner of Sir Dedlock. The Ironmaster, Mrs Rouncewell's 'industrious apprentice' son and a Napoleon of industry, visits Chesney Wold. He too has been elected to Parliament. Sir Leicester sees it as an omen of apocalyptic significance: 'the floodgates of society are burst open'. While the company are still assembled after the election (won by Sir Thomas Doodle, despite the floodgates being burst), Tulkinghorn comes to Chesney Wold. In company, he tells a lightly veiled version of Lady Dedlock's story. More of her background emerges and we discover that she was the daughter of a townsman of the Ironmaster (she came from the north, which might explain why she has no immediately accessible family). The young Lady Dedlock (we still do not know her first name), was taken up by a 'great lady' (just like Rosa), and became engaged to marry a captain in the army (a 'young rake'). She did not, in fact marry him, but bore his child. The captain having since died, she thought herself safe, but as the remorseless Tulkinghorn warns, she is not.

None of the other Dedlocks, or their hangers-on, appreciate exactly what Tulkinghorn is telling them. Lady Dedlock, however, does. She is entirely in the lawyer's power, as he stresses in a subsequent private exchange. She intimates her intention to leave Chesney Wold and disappear, but he dissuades her, much as he enjoys playing cat-and-mouse with Lady Dedlock, he does not want to lose his client, Sir Leicester. She is to remain, but always under the control of Mr Tulkinghorn.

On his return to London, Tulkinghorn is visited by Snagsby, who has been much put out by a visit from Hortense, who is still hovering, sinisterly, on the edge of things. Guster has been provoked into fits. The Frenchwoman wishes to have an interview with Tulkinghorn, but he has declined to see her. However, he now summonses the pertinacious Frenchwoman to his chambers. 'I hate my Lady', she tells him. Tulkinghorn threatens her with prison: 'In this city, there are houses of correction (where the treadmills are, for women) the gates of which are very strong and heavy'. She leaves, fulminating hatred for Tulkinghorn as well as her former mistress. The number ends, enigmatically, with the figure of 'Allegory' on the lawyer's ceiling pointing to who knows where.

*

Why does Dickens so hate the law?

Viewed objectively, the fact that Britain in the nineteenth century became increasingly a lawful society is entirely a good thing. Nonetheless, few members of any society, however orderly, have good words to say about lawyers. There are, in 2005, websites devoted to lawyer jokes – invariably bitter (e.g. 'How do you know when a lawyer is lying?' 'His lips move'). 'Finding a good lawyer in Dickens's fiction' is almost as hard as finding a good landlord in contemporary fiction. For the occasional Mr Wickfield (a very feeble good lawyer), there are three or four Uriah Heeps, or bullying Mr Jaggers. As a matter of principle, Dickens hated 'systems', particularly bureaucratic systems (it was civil service bureaucracy, he believed, which led to the Crimean War fiasco). He never saw a piece of red tape he did not want to cut, and British law is swathed with the stuff.

Dickens's dislike of pettifogging lawyers may have a personal origin. He was himself once a solicitor's clerk (like the extremely odious Guppy), and evidently disliked it as much as the blacking factory to which he was cruelly sent as a little boy. His family's bankruptcy and the legal contracts ('bills') that initiated it, may have predisposed young Charles to hate the law. So, I suspect, did the morass of contracts which he signed after the runaway success of *Pickwick Papers*. He was obliged to buy himself out of them and – most insulting – to buy back the copyright of his own published work.

The emblem of English law in *Bleak House* is less the icy villain Tulkinghorn (who seems to have walked into Victorian fiction from the Jacobean stage), than the bloodsucking leech, Vholes. Lawyers at the time objected that Dickens's representation of English Law in *Bleak House* was biased. They would, though, wouldn't they?

Dickens and party politics

The thirteenth number is dominated by a General Election. Dickens has as little reverence for the glories of British democracy as for the dignity of British law. The election is a battle between Mr Coodle and Sir Thomas Doodle (from the title, we gather he represents the Tory interest) Sir Leicester Dedlock, representing, of course, his own corrupt borough, is with the Doodleites (Thomasite faction). In addition to his own unopposed seat, he has 'two other little seats that belong to him' – that is boroughs in which he, as landlord, controls the vote. He is outraged that the Doodleite victory has cost the party 'hundreds of thousands of pounds' in bribes.

Dickens despised the pre-1867 reform system, with its restricted franchise, public voting, nepotistic appointments and open bribery. Nor, as the names Coodle and Doodle indicate, did he see any great difference between the Liberal, Whig and Conservative parties. What was lacking, clearly, was radicalism, and unfortunately for Dickens there would not be any organised radicalism until long after his death and the emergence of the Independent Labour Party and the general franchise (although whether Dickens would have approved of women voting is debatable).

Dickens's satire on the manifest corruption of 'pocket boroughs' doubtless added some force to the reform movement that would abolish Dedlock-style corruption forever in 1867. Sir Leicester's gratification at the success of 'our party' is blemished by the discovery that the Ironmaster (assisted by his son), has been elected to a constituency in the north. That vibrantly industrial region, with its huge conurbations and newly enriched captains of industry, is not to be bullied by landlords or bought with sovereigns and pints of beer. Sir Leicester's response to the Ironmaster joining him in the House is Biblical – apocalypse is nigh:

> 'Then upon my honour,' says Sir Leicester after a terrific pause, during which he has been heard to snort and felt to stare; 'then upon my honour, upon my life, upon my reputation and principles, the floodgates of society are burst open, and the waters have – a – obliterated the landmarks of the framework of the cohesion by which things are held together!'

Power is indeed shifting from the landed gentry to the factories. Does Dickens approve? Yes, it would seem so.

Plate 31. Sir Leicester Dedlock

*

Instalment 14 (Chapters 43–46),
April 1853

Summary

Esther is now very much at the centre of things at Bleak House, and occasionally in the townhouse in London (where she once, accidentally, sees her mother at the theatre). She and John Jarndyce are worried by the malign influence that Skimpole is having on Richard, and they visit the 'child' in his apartments in Somers Town. He, of course, is applying himself to devouring delicacies, sipping good wine, and paying for nothing. He is, when they arrive, contemplating his wallflowers and having fine thoughts.

Esther has her first meeting with Skimpole's three daughters, representing between them the spirits of Beauty, Sentiment, and Comedy. The long-suffering Mrs Skimpole is neither beautiful nor sentimental, but, like everything in this household, very comic. All the Skimpole sons (wisely) ran away as soon as they were old enough to run. As usual, Skimpole deflects the plea that he cease pillaging Richard, on the irrefutable grounds of his innocence of the ways of the world.

Esther, Richard and Skimpole make their way to Bleak House where, they are called on by Sir Leicester Dedlock. He graciously apologises for having been less civil to John Jarndyce than he could have been (he has learnt of his distant relationship to Lady Dedlock through the case). He is also at pains to offer his lordly assistance to Skimpole, who has indicated a desire to cast his eye over the fine art at Chesney Wold. Sir Leicester also adverts to the obnoxious Boythorn, with whom he is at law.

Esther is much disturbed by the visit of the 'Great Lincolnshire baronet', who is, of course, in a sense her stepfather. After he has gone, John Jarndyce vouchsafes more of the background to Esther's birth. Boythorn had been in love with Lady Dedlock's sister, Esther's aunt. After taking in (or taking away) Esther, the woman's heart hardened and she cut off all relations with Boythorn. Esther explains to her guardian that her godmother was the sister of Lady Dedlock. Now all the pieces (bar Hawdon's role), fit.

The next day, John Jarndyce and Esther have a council of war. What dangerous outsiders, they ask themselves, know the 'secret'? Tulkinghorn, Guppy, and perhaps the French maid, Hortense, who has been acting very suspiciously and frighteningly. Now that he knows the full story of Esther's 'inheritance of shame', John Jarndyce takes a decisive step. He sends her a letter, offering marriage, or, as Esther puts it, the owner of Bleak House asks her if she would 'be the mistress of Bleak House'. He would not, she shrewdly suspects, have asked her were she still a beauty. After some dilemma, Esther burns the now dried flowers that Allan Woodcourt left her and accepts her guardian's offer. They agree to wait, making no public announcement, and speak no more of the matter between themselves. This number is mainly told in Esther's voice and narration; she is now, clearly, the centre of the novel.

Vholes, forever sucking Richard's life-blood, warns that the young man's funds (the attorney's income, that is), are drying up. Charley and Esther make a journey down to Deal, on the coast, where Richard is staying. He tells them that he intends to sell his commission. Like all the other professions, soldiering has not worked; worse than that, he is on the brink of disgrace, as army officers are not privileged to bankrupt themselves. Esther has brought with her a letter in which Ada offers Richard, whom she still loves, her 'little inheritance'. He has enough honour left in him to refuse. He will not give up the case and he will not relent in his hatred towards John Jarndyce. Esther sadly realises that her trip has been a failure.

But there is one accidental outcome which will be important to her. An 'Indiaman' trading ship has docked. Its surgeon, Esther discovers, is Allan Woodcourt. After some mental turmoil and with a veil covering her disfigured face, she resolves to see the man that she will now, she believes, never marry. She wants the situation to be clear and to ensure that he will not nurture any false hopes. Despite his heroics in the shipwreck, India has not worked for him, and Allan Woodcourt has not risen in his profession. He clearly feels for Esther and for her sake, promises to befriend Richard whom he has seen in Deal, and observed to be in a condition of 'ungrown despair' – on the brink of suicide (one of the principal causes of death in this novel).

Returned to London, Woodcourt has other old friends to catch up on. Patrolling, as is his wont, the slum streets around Tom-all-Alone's, he comes across Jenny, the brickmaker's wife, who has been beaten by her husband and he tends her wounds. We learn that the family are on the tramp again. Woodcourt also comes across Jo – whom he first met at Nemo's Inquest. The boy is in a sorry state – 'haunted', as he says, and longing for death. Since his encounter with Lady Dedlock (masquerading as Hortense) at Nemo's 'berryin place', he has been forever chivvied. A mysterious someone (Bucket, working for Tulkinghorn), gave him four half-crowns on his discharge from hospital (after his flight from Bleak

House, leaving the smallpox behind him), with the stern instruction that he 'move on'. Forever. Woodcourt resolves to take care of the waif. He need move no more.

*

Dating confusion. Again.

When John Jarndyce and Esther visit Skimpole at his London apartments in the Polygon, in Somers Town (just north of St Pancras in modern London), there are, in the environs, a number of 'poor Spanish refugees walking about in cloaks, smoking little paper cigars' (probably the first reference to cigarettes in English fiction). These Spaniards have been identified as exiles, rebels under General Torrijos, who failed to overthrow their government in 1831. Does this mean the action has, at last, been given a firm time setting? A little later on, Esther says that 'in those coach days', it takes nine hours to get from London to the coastal town of Deal (a journey which the young Dickens, living among the dockyards, would have known well). That, too, would suggest a date in the early 1830s, before train travel (which spread rapidly all over England in the 1840s). In Chapter 55 (still to come), Dickens notes that:

> Railroads shall soon traverse all this country, and with a rattle and a glare the engine and train shall shoot like a meteor over the wide night-landscape, turning the moon paler; but as yet, such things are non-existent in these parts, though not wholly unexpected. Preparations are afoot, measurements are made, ground is staked out. Bridges are begun, and their not yet united piers desolately look at one another over roads and streams, like brick and mortar couples with an obstacle to their union; fragments of embankments are thrown up, and left as precipices with torrents of rusty carts and barrows tumbling

over them; tripods of tall poles appear on hill-tops, where there are rumours of tunnels; everything looks chaotic, and abandoned in full hopelessness. Along the freezing roads, and through the night, the post-chaise makes its way without a railroad on its mind.

Here again we would deduce a setting of the mid-1830s. It would be convenient to attach a date to the narrative, but other references (to the post-1839 Post Office, the telegraph, or Bucket's journey to Lincolnshire by train later in the action, for example), won't allow it. We have to assume multiple time settings for the action with a central era of, most probably, the 1840s. It is, of course, a major problem for the TV adaptation which – unlike Dr Who on his recent Victorian escapades – does not have the luxury of travelling backwards and forwards in time.

What is the deadliest of Dickensian sins?

The deadliest of Dickensian sins is, without question, 'hypocrisy'. False appearance – pretending to be something (typically something highly virtuous) that you are not, is the cardinal offence. The arch-hypocrite in *Bleak House* is Harold Skimpole. In reply to John Jarndyce's observation, for example, that they must spare Richard's pocket, Skimpole replies:

> 'My dear Jarndyce,' returned Mr Skimpole, 'I will do anything to give you pleasure, but it seems an idle form – a superstition. Besides, I give you my word, Miss Clare and my dear Miss Summerson, I thought Mr Carstone was immensely rich. I thought he had only to make over something, or to sign a bond, or a draft, or a cheque, or a bill, or to put something on a file somewhere, to bring down a shower of money.'
> 'Indeed it is not so, sir,' said Ada. 'He is poor.'

> 'No, really?' returned Mr Skimpole, with his bright smile, 'you surprise me.'

Is he in fact surprised? Not at all. As the novel progresses we appreciate that he is an arch, supremely self-serving, hypocrite. Esther, increasingly, sees through Skimpole. John Jarndyce in a mark of *his* truly childish innocence, obstinately does not. He persists in seeing Harold Skimpole for what he hypocritically pretends to be, a child. Why did the Victorians (not just Dickens) so hate hypocrisy? Because, one might suggest, theirs was a society based, above all, on moral values. The hypocrite was a kind of moral embezzler. Hypocrisy debased the currency on which their society was founded. Ours, as the financial supplements confirm, is founded on a different currency.

Who knew what, when?

After Sir Leicester's visit, John Jarndyce explains yet another aspect to the vexed and increasingly curious circumstances of Esther's birth and upbringing. Boythorn, it emerges, had been in love with Lady Dedlock's sister before the two ladies separated. The failure of the affair has blighted his life and turned him into the monster of comic wrath (and inveterate foe of Sir Leicester), that he is. After the strange business of the birth, 'death', and adoption of Esther by her 'godmother', all relations between the lovers, Boythorn and Esther's aunt, were cut off. By her.

As John Jarndyce puts it:

> 'It was her act, and she kept its motives in her inflexible heart. He afterwards did conjecture (but it was mere conjecture), that some injury which her haughty spirit had received in her cause

of quarrel with her sister, had wounded her beyond all reason; but she wrote him that from the date of that letter she died to him – as in literal truth she did – and that the resolution was exacted from her by her knowledge of his proud temper and his strained sense of honour, which were both her nature too. In consideration for those master points in him, and even in consideration for them in herself, she made the sacrifice, she said, and would live in it and die in it. She did both, I fear: certainly he never saw her, never heard of her from that hour. Nor did any one.'

This reawakens familiar curiosity in the reader/viewer. Who was commissioning Kenge to make Esther's child support payments? Is it likely that Boythorn, who must have known the young Lady Dedlock when she was plain Miss Honoria Nobody, would not recognise her now (every one else seems to be well up on the family resemblance with Esther, for example)? He is her neighbour and must see her every week at church when the Dedlocks are at their place in Lincolnshire. Is it plausible that some leakage as to the true facts would have slipped out over the years (Mrs Chadband, née Rachael, is clearly not a paragon of discretion)?

Even more surprising is the fact that John Jarndyce needs to be informed by Rachael that Esther's godmother and Lady Dedlock are sisters: 'Yes, guardian, yes! And *her* sister is my mother'. It is clear, from their conversation in the rainstorm, that he knew both sisters in the old days, and, presumably, knew the family. It is clear too, that if Lady Dedlock is involved in the Jarndyce case, so most likely is her sister. A whole gaggle of lawyers, not bound by Kenge's seal of secrecy to his client, would be in the know. Even the Ironmaster, it seems, may have known, or known of, the Barbary sisters.

Why is Allan Woodcourt such an unsuccessful physician? Or is he?

Unlike the comfortably well-off Bayham Badger, Allan Woodcourt seems, despite his manifest intelligence, diligence, and excellent medical training at Edinburgh University, to be the least thriving of doctors. When Esther is re-united with him, on his return from the East, he tells her that it is doubtful he will return to India:

> He had not found himself more favoured by fortune there than here. He had gone out a poor ship's surgeon, and had come home nothing better.

Back in London, he is similarly disfavoured by fortune. It is not, apparently, that he is a bad doctor. His failure to rise in the world seems connected with his incorrigible philanthropy. He insists on treating (and paying for the medicine for) indigent patients: Nemo, Jo, Miss Flite, Jenny. There could not be a poor person that would not find a friend in Woodcourt. In India, one cannot doubt, he attended on the natives rather than the maharajahs. In London, as we note, he prowls the streets looking for down-and-outs to minister to. Not to spoil the story, he never rises high in his profession. The point Dickens seems to be making is that he bestows his healing gift where it is most needed (not, for example, on Sir Leicester's gout, or Mr Vholes's indigestion). He is medical goodness incarnate: like the mendicant friar, he has taken poverty as the inevitable companion of his vocation. Finally John Jarndyce finds a place for him attending the poor, for a gentleman's salary, in Yorkshire. The post is, Jarndyce says, appropriate for such a man:

'I mean, a man whose hopes and aims may sometimes lie (as most men's sometimes do, I dare say) above the ordinary level, but to whom the ordinary level will be high enough after all, if it should prove to be a way of usefulness and good service leading to no other. All generous spirits are ambitious, I suppose; but the ambition that calmly trusts itself to such a road, instead of spasmodically trying to fly over it, is of the kind I care for. It is Woodcourt's kind.'

Unremunerated as he may be, Woodcourt is, we deduce, the best of physicians. Would that there were lawyers like him.

Why repair the slums?

The slums must be repaired, because, Dickens argues, with one of his most florid sermonettes, if you don't repair the slums the slums will come and get you – in however grand a mansion you reside. Tom-all-Alone's, if left alone, will have its revenge:

> Even the winds are his messengers, and they serve him in these hours of darkness. There is not a drop of Tom's corrupted blood but propagates infection and contagion somewhere ... There is not an atom of Tom's slime, not a cubic inch of any pestilential gas in which he lives, not one obscenity or degradation about him, not an ignorance, not a wickedness, not a brutality of his committing, but shall work its retribution, through every order of society, up to the proudest of the proud, and to the highest of the high. Verily, what with tainting, plundering, and spoiling, Tom has his revenge.

As in the earlier dark rhapsodies on the fog, Dickens here alludes to that Victorian belief in disease aetiology – the miasmic theory. Smallpox, typhus, a multitude of deadly fevers are borne on airborne currents. The sentiment and rhetoric are Carlylean. Sanitation is not philanthropy, it is self-interest.

One of the persistent mysteries is the hint that John Jarndyce is the landlord of Tom-all-Alone's. Why does he not convert it into model apartments for the deserving poor?

*

Instalment 15 (Chapters 47–49),
May 1853

Summary

Allan has taken charge of the sick Jo, but where can he lodge the boy? After consulting his old client Miss Flite, he resolves to take him to George's shooting gallery. Like Woodcourt, an unfailing friend to the friendless (Phil Squod, for example), George takes him in, partly, as he says, because of his high regard for Miss Summerson. Phil, like Guster before him and having also been found in the gutter, is kind to Jo, who slowly dies over the next few days, visited by Esther and Snagsby and cared for by Woodcourt. To the end, the boy is racked with guilt that he it was who infected Esther. His death enrages George still further against the callous Tulkinghorn. He unwisely goes so far as to threaten violence. Jo dies in a furnace of pathos and Dickensian sentimentality.

Meanwhile, the Dedlocks are in town. Lady Dedlock, aware that her enemies are 'closing in' around her, resolves to dismiss Rosa so that the girl will be free to marry Watt Rouncewell. She does not want the 'timid little beauty' whom she has adopted to suffer the same things that happened in her own youth'. The Ironmaster is summoned and agrees to take charge of the girl on his son's behalf. Watt, it seems, still loves Rosa (Dickens does not invest much description in this sub-plot, which serves only to contextualise Lady Dedlock's past).

Tulkinghorn happens to be present. He interprets Lady Dedlock's benevolent act as a contravention of their 'agreement' (i.e. he is to make all the decisions in her life as if she were his puppet). He gives her to understand that, when it suits him, he will denounce her to Sir Leicester and the world. Despite a series of ill omens, Tulkinghorn returns to his chambers, coldly satisfied with his evening's work. Meanwhile Lady Dedlock, gowned and veiled as is her wont, slips out of the town house. A gunshot is heard. Underneath the ceiling depiction of the allegorical Roman with his pointing finger, the next morning the room cleaner discovers Tulkinghorn 'lying face downward on the floor, shot through the heart.' Like the Roman, Dickens has pointed the finger at two suspects: George and Lady Dedlock. Whodunnit?

The scene switches abruptly to the Bagnet household. It is Mrs Bagnet's birthday, a red-letter day in the annual calendar. Bagnet and the children cook the meal and do the housework. Trooper George comes to join the celebrations and so, surprisingly, does Inspector Bucket, who charms the company. On leaving however, his real motive emerges. George is arrested, handcuffed, and taken off to prison on suspicion of having murdered Mr Tulkinghorn. 'Great Heaven', he ejaculates, 'I was there, last night', protesting his innocence. But why on earth was he there?

*

The big issue: what to do with the street people

With mass urbanization and the lack of anything resembling a welfare state other than a parochial charity system originally devised for Elizabethan England, the Victorians were at a loss as to what to do with their 'excluded' (as New Labour would call them). Dickens dramatises the problem in Woodcourt's dilemma of what he should do with the dying Jo. He and George debate the problem:

> 'And, Mr George, I am in this difficulty about him. I am unwilling to place him in a hospital, even if I could procure him immediate admission, because I foresee that he would not stay there many hours, if he could be so much as got there. The same objection applies to a workhouse; supposing I had the patience to be evaded and shirked, and handed about from post to pillar in trying to get him into one – which is a system that I don't take kindly to.'
>
> 'No man does, sir,' returns Mr George.

Dickens certainly didn't take kindly to workhouses, as *Oliver Twist* makes clear, but what could replace them? Dickens seems to have believed in 'doing the best that you could' – as he himself was doing with Urania Cottage. It didn't come near solving the problem of metropolitan prostitution, but it solved the problem for the small number of 'fallen' girls that he and Miss Burdett-Coutts took in from the many thousands doomed to continue walking the streets. So too do the good-hearted Allan and George do the best that they can. They solve Jo's problem of where, comfortably, he may die. It doesn't help the thousands of children sleeping rough, but it does help. Microcharity, one might call it. From a macroeconomic perspective, Dickens believed that the vast sums raised to convert the heathen abroad might be usefully diverted to helping unfortunates nearer home. In fact, he becomes something of a nag on the subject in *Bleak House*, giving us in this number yet another lecture cum sermon on the subject:

> Jo is brought in. He is not one of Mrs Pardiggle's Tockahoopo Indians; he is not one of Mrs Jellyby's lambs, being wholly unconnected with Borrioboola-Gha; he is not softened by dis-

tance and unfamiliarity; he is not a genuine foreign-grown savage; he is the ordinary home-made article. Dirty, ugly, disagreeable to all the senses, in body a common creature of the common streets, only in soul a heathen. Homely filth begrimes him, homely parasites devour him, homely sores are in him, homely rags are on him: native ignorance, the growth of English soil and climate, sinks his immortal nature lower than the beasts that perish. Stand forth, Jo, in uncompromising colours! From the sole of thy foot to the crown of thy head, there is nothing interesting about thee.

As is typical when he is aroused, Dickens's novelist mask slips and he is here addressing (or hectoring) the reader *in propria persona*. Forget the novel.

Why does Jo 'Sir' his way to eternity?

The death of Jo the street sweep, along with that of Little Nell and Paul Dombey (in *The Old Curiosity Shop* and *Dombey and Son* respectively), is one of the most tremendous achievements of Dickensian pathos. It is, however, much more than a tearjerker. Jo tells Woodcourt, who is ministering – part doctor, part lay priest – to the boy's last moments that he wishes to be buried alongside 'him as wos wery good to me'. Hawdon/Nemo, that is:

'It's time for me to go to that there berryin ground, sir,' he returns with a wild look.
'Lie down, and tell me. What burying ground, Jo?'
'Where they laid him as wos wery good to me, wery good to me indeed, he wos. It's time fur me to go down to that there berryin ground, sir, and ask to be put along with him. I wants to go there and be berried. He used fur to say to me, "I am as poor as you today, Jo," he ses. I wants to tell him that I am as

poor as him now, and have come there to be laid along with him.'

'Bye and bye, Jo. Bye and bye.'

'Ah! P'raps they wouldn't do it if I wos to go myself. But will you promise to have me took there, sir, and laid along with him?'

'I will, indeed.'

'Thankee, sir. Thankee, sir. They'll have to get the key of the gate afore they can take me in, for it's allus locked. And there's a step there, as I used for to clean with my broom. – It's turned wery dark, sir. Is there any light a comin?'

'It is coming fast, Jo.'

Fast. The cart is shaken all to pieces, and the rugged road is very near its end.

'Jo, my poor fellow!'

'I hear you, sir, in the dark, but I'm a gropin – a gropin – let me catch hold of your hand.'

'Jo, can you say what I say?'

'I'll say anythink as you say, sir, for I knows it's good.'

'OUR FATHER.'

'Our Father! – Yes, that's wery good, sir.'

'WHICH ART IN HEAVEN.'

'Art in Heaven – is the light a comin, sir?'

'It is close at hand. HALLOWED BE THY NAME!'

'Hallowed be – thy –'

The light is come upon the dark benighted way. Dead!

Dead, your Majesty. Dead, my lords and gentlemen. Dead, Right Reverends and Wrong Reverends of every order. Dead, men and women, born with Heavenly compassion in your hearts. And dying thus around us, every day.

Jo does not know that minimum of Christian teaching, the Lord's Prayer. Ignorance of it previously disqualified him from testifying at the inquest. Will it disqualify him from entrance into heaven? What is remarkable in this passage, to the modern ear, is the repetition of the word 'sir'. Jo does not, of course, sir 'Mr Sangsby', who is of lower professional caste than Dr Woodcourt. He may be a street urchin, but he knows the fine distinctions of Victorian rank.

The point Dickens seems to be making with all this death-bed 'sirring' is that, if well-treated, the poor are not revolutionary, not violent, not brutish. They know their place and are deferential. Doubtless, when he gets to the pearly gates, Jo will address Saint Peter as sir seven times over, just as he does Woodcourt. The other point, of course, is that unlike Sir Leicester Dedlock, Allan deserves the appellation 'Sir'. The final apostrophe, delivered full frontal to the reader, contains one of the most astonishing pieces of *lèse majesté* in Victorian fiction: 'Dead, your Majesty. Dead, my lords and Gentlemen'. Dickens indicts, hierarchically, the Queen of England, the House of Lords, the House of Commons, the Church of England – and, of course, the reader of *Bleak House*. This, I think, is the only *ad feminam* accusation against Queen Victoria to be found in the canon of respectable Victorian fiction. And a very angry accusation it is.

Who *is* Jo's father?

Mrs Snagsby has no doubt that it is her gadabout husband who cannot see the boy without giving him a half-crown – proof enough, in her eyes, but the meek stationer is, to a certainty, not the guilty parent. Dickens, who has so tantalised the reader over so many months about Esther's parentage, refuses to concoct a melodramatic back story for Jo, although he could very easily have done so. He dies fatherless – reciting, for the first time in his life, 'Our Father'. Jo wants to be buried (filthy as the place is) alongside 'him as wos wery good to me', Hawdon: the fellow destitute who has adopted him. It would have been a simple stroke of the pen for Dickens to have made Hawdon, who has fathered one bastard already, Jo's father. But he forbore. Jo is literally what Hawdon tried to be, a 'no-one', a child of the gutter. It is a fine example of Dickensian restraint – not something he is often credited with.

*

Instalment 16 (Chapters 50–53),

June 1853

Summary

Esther goes to stay with Caddy, who has had a child – a very sickly child – named, of course, Esther. Always a friend to those unable to pay his fee (or a large fee), Caddy and her sickly infant are being attended by Allan Woodcourt. Since Esther and John Jarndyce resolved to keep their engagement secret, he does not seem to know that she is betrothed. Some remarks of John Jarndyce's to Esther concerning Allan's income suggest that he, in his benevolence, has observed the still existing bond between them, and is not disposed to force Esther into a relationship she may not, in the last analysis, want with her guardian-fiancée. Ada is coming up to twenty-one years of age, at which point she will no longer be a ward of court. She will be mistress of her own (modest) property, and free, should she wish, to marry, without either the court or her guardian's consent. Esther notices, without paying much attention, that Ada keeps her left hand hidden under the pillow at night when, having locked up the house, it is Dame Durden's last act to kiss her 'dear girl' goodnight.

Woodcourt calls on Carstone in his lodgings alongside Vholes's chambers. The young man remains obsessed with the case and says, enigmatically, that Ada's interests 'are bound up with mine'. On a visit to Richard with Ada, Esther is told that her two friends have been married 'above two months'. That is, they married shortly before Ada came of age, although now that she is of age, they cannot be separated. Her motive, she said, was to persuade him to accept her money. She intends, henceforth, to live publicly with her husband, alongside Vholes's chambers. John Jarndyce, as ever, takes the news with generous sadness.

Esther and Jarndyce learn that Tulkinghorn has been murdered and George arrested. It could be dangerous if 'secrets' came out in the investigation and trial. They believe George's protestation that he is innocent of the crime and visit him in prison. He fiercely resists John Jarndyce's offer to get him a lawyer. He does not trust them, nor, of course, does he want *his* secrets to come out. The Bagnets also visit the prison. The 'old girl', with her sharp woman's eye, noted earlier how upset George was by the sight of Mrs Rouncewell, and has (correctly) deduced who the mother was, whose hair he whitened. She stumps off, umbrella in hand, to fetch the housekeeper from Chesney Wold. The number ends with Bucket establishing that Lady Dedlock left her London house, veiled and gowned (as usual) shortly before the murder. The finger of suspicion is turning her way.

*

Why does Ada marry Richard?

Ada's motive for marrying Richard (without John Jarndyce's consent) is that, she says:

> 'All I had was Richard's,' Ada said; 'and Richard would not take it, Esther, and what could I do but be his wife when I loved him dearly!'
> 'And you were so fully and so kindly occupied, excellent Dame Durden,' said Richard, 'that how could we speak to you

at such a time! And besides, it was not a long-considered step. We went out one morning, and were married.'

Ada has kept it secret, presumably, because she was not quite, at that point, of age. When, one might idly wonder, was the marriage consummated? Or is it on this night when she resolves to stay with Richard that it will be consummated, some two months after the ceremony? Where were the banns called? And did nobody notice? By unreformed Victorian law (unreformed, that is, until the 1880s), the wife's property and wealth, unless specifically protected by legal contract, belonged to the husband. Richard now has no choice but to accept ownership of it. But why did he marry a woman whom he has no means of supporting? Did Richard, at the prompting of Vholes, either acquiesce or even encourage Ada's reckless act?

It could mean, of course, that she is cut out of John Jarndyce's will (he will not want *his* money to be siphoned, via Richard and Vholes, into the insatiable maw of the 'case'). The act is dishonourable on Richard's part, and a clear indication of the moral decay which is accompanying his financial ruin.

Make 'em wait

Dickens loved playing cat-and-mouse with the reader. Having set up George as the likely murder suspect he then (when George stoutly protests his innocence), diverts our suspicion to the other person we know to have been out on the streets, around Lincoln's Inn, at ten o'clock on the fateful night of the murder. When Esther and John Jarndyce visit George in prison, he observes:

[Esther's] height and figure, which seemed to catch his attention all at once.

''Tis curious,' said he. 'And yet I thought so at the time!'

My guardian asked him what he meant.

'Why, sir,' he answered, 'when my ill-fortune took me to the dead man's staircase on the night of his murder, I saw a shape so like Miss Summerson's go by me in the dark, that I had half a mind to speak to it.'

For an instant, I felt such a shudder as I never felt before or since, and hope I shall never feel again.

We know that the murderer/murderess was not Esther. Was it then the woman whom she resembles most in the world – Lady Dedlock? Bucket, we learn, is receiving anonymous letters containing the words: 'Lady Dedlock', but we do not know who is sending them. The detective has discovered, by the subtle interrogation of a Dedlock footman, that Lady Dedlock left the London house, heavily veiled, shortly before the murder. On an earlier occasion, when Tulkinghorn was present, a gunshot was heard distantly at Chesney Wold. Lady Dedlock could have brought up a firearm with her from the country in her capacious luggage.

Do we 'like' Bucket?

Bucket can claim to be the first detective proper in English fiction (bringing with him much of the machinery of what we are now familiar with in the crime fiction genre). He is an enigmatic character; with his fat forefinger, his false bonhomie, his omniscience and his indifference to everything other than solving the crime, he is also a somewhat sinister figure. And he is ruthless. He is, for example, prepared to use his own wife as a lure (by taking in Hortense as a lodger).

It becomes clear that Bucket does not think, probably never

Plate 32. Friendly Behaviour of Mr Bucket

has thought George the perpetrator – but he is prepared to imprison him (with repeated remand orders) in order to entrap the true culprit. The fact that, in prison, George cannot pay his creditors and will be sold up (with the Bagnets) is of no interest to Bucket.

The detective's revelation to Sir Leicester that his wife may be the perpetrator and is certainly the mother of an illegitimate child, verges on the sadistic. The theatrical denouement scene, (much imitated by later crime writers) is inhuman. He is, as Hortense repeatedly says, a 'devil', but he is also devilishly clever. Bucket is, among his many parts, a premonitory manifestation of what the twentieth century would recognise as the police state. There is, for example, a scene later in the novel where Esther observes him gathering intelligence in London:

Sometimes we emerged upon a wider thoroughfare, or came to a larger building than the generality, well lighted. Then we stopped at offices like those we had visited when we began our journey, and I saw him in consultation with others. Sometimes he would get down by an archway, or at a street corner, and mysteriously show the light of his little lantern. This would attract similar lights from various dark quarters, like so many insects, and a fresh consultation would be held. By degrees we appeared to contract our search within narrower and easier limits. Single police-officers on duty could now tell Mr Bucket what he wanted to know, and point to him where to go. At last we stopped for a rather long conversation between him and one of these men, which I supposed to be satisfactory from his manner of nodding from time to time. When it was finished he came to me, looking very busy and very attentive.

Bucket has his men everywhere – in uniform and plain clothes – his eyes never sleep. Beria, Edgar J. Hoover, the Stasi. All are implicit in the depiction of Inspector Bucket. But so too is Inspector Morse.

*

Instalment 17 (Chapters 54–56),

July 1853

Summary

Bucket calls on Sir Leicester Dedlock to reveal to him the murderer, and to earn the £100 reward the baronet has offered him. He is, of course, employed by Sir Leicester (as a 'confidential agent'), as well as by the London Detective Service, and owes the baronet first knowledge of what he has discovered. The perpetrator was, he tells the astonished baronet, 'a woman'. In a long denouement scene, he reveals the entire secret history of Lady Dedlock. She, he says, 'is the pivot it all turns on'. An appalled Sir Leicester learns of the illicit association with Hawdon, the man who 'was her lover long before you courted her, and who ought to have been her husband'. Esther's name, however, does not come up at this point (does Bucket know about her?).

The Smallweeds, Snagsby and Mrs Chadband are summoned. The incriminating letters (not, apparently, destroyed after all), are displayed. The Smallweeds want £500 for them. There is some squalid haggling and, as the tension reaches unbearable levels, Mr Bucket unmasks the murder / murderess. It is neither of the obvious suspects, but Hortense – Lady Dedlock's former maid, who has been lodging (most improbably) with the Buckets. A *coup de foudre*, as the lady's countrymen would say. It turns out that Bucket imprisoned George simply to lull his true suspect into a sense of false security. It is Hortense who has been sending the poison pen

205

letters to Bucket – from Bucket's own household! She committed the crime with a pocket pistol. With much baring of teeth, Hortense is handcuffed and led away. Newgate and the gallows await.

Clearly there is nothing left for Lady Dedlock but flight, oblivion and perhaps, death. Rather clumsily, in Chapter 55, Dickens goes back in time to a period shortly before the resolution of the mystery, when 'the detective has not yet struck his great blow', while George is still in prison as the main suspect and Hortense's guilt is, as yet, undisclosed. The redoubtable Mrs Bagnet has brought back Mrs Rouncewell from Lincolnshire. George is reunited with his mother in his cell and tears are soon flowing. He accepts her forgiveness, but demands that she does not reveal his whereabouts to his wealthy brother. Mrs Rouncewell has received a letter accusing her mistress of being a murderess and takes it to Lady Dedlock, pleading with her to 'confess'. Guppy, her former tormentor, appears after Mrs Rouncewell has left. He too, as he cagily implies, knows her secret. The letters were not, after all, destroyed by the spontaneous combustion.

After Guppy has left, she writes a farewell note for Sir Leicester (confessing everything except the murder of which 'I am wholly innocent'), and flees the town house, leaving all her jewels and money. She does not know that Sir Leicester has fallen victim to a stroke and will never be able to read her letter. Her absence is discovered the next morning by Volumnia. Bucket is summoned and a 'pursuit' mounted. Sir Leicester, who cannot speak, scrawls on a slate: 'Full forgiveness. Find —'. Bucket searches her boudoir and is surprised to find that she has taken nothing with her. He finds in her dresser a handkerchief with the name 'Esther Summerson' embroidered on it (the same piece of linen that Lady Dedlock bought from the brickmakers, as a souvenir of her daughter). Perhaps, thinks Bucket, that is where Lady Dedlock will have gone. Esther now joins him in the pursuit. The chase is on, but where has Lady Dedlock fled to?

*

How good a crime novelist is Dickens?

Inventing, as he is, much of the machinery of crime fiction, Dickens is not always smooth in operating it. Parts of the murder and detection plot creak painfully. The fact, for example, that there were no less than three people on Tulkinghorn's staircase, shortly before ten o'clock when he was murdered, strains credulity. They all had a motive to kill the lawyer, but only one of them had a motive to be there. Why did George go to the lawyer's chambers? Was it to upbraid him with the death of Jo? Why was Lady Dedlock there – to plead with him for more time, or for mercy? Why did Hortense kill him – to implicate Lady Dedlock, whom she hates, or to settle a score with Tulkinghorn, whom she equally hates? If she killed all the people she hated, the passionate Frenchwoman would need a Gatling gun, not a pocket pistol. Where did she get her pistol? Why, of all people in London, would Hortense take up lodgings with the police officer investigating the murder she committed? Why not flee to France and safety? Is it plausible that Tulkinghorn, one of the richest and most eminent lawyers in London (honoured with what is virtually a state funeral), would not have had some servant in the house at ten o'clock ? Does he light his own candles, pour his own sherry, lay out his own bed? Empty his own chamber pot? We are, frankly, in Swiss cheese territory. Holes everywhere.

What *is* Lady Dedlock's christian name?

Finally, when the Smallweeds triumphantly produce the packet of Lady Dedlock's incriminating letters to Hawdon, we learn what Lady Dedlock's first name is. It is ironic, needless to say:

> 'I was the client and friend of Mr Tulkinghorn,' pipes Grandfather Smallweed then; 'I did business with him. I was useful to him, and he was useful to me. Krook, dead and gone, was my brother-in-law. He was own brother to a brimstone magpie – leastways Mrs Smallweed. I come into Krook's property. I examined all his papers and all his effects. They was all dug out under my eyes. There was a bundle of letters belonging to a dead and gone lodger, as was hid away at the back of a shelf in the side of Lady Jane's bed – his cat's bed. He hid all manner of things away, everywheres. Mr Tulkinghorn wanted 'em and got 'em, but I looked 'em over first. I'm a man of business, and I took a squint at 'em. They was letters from the lodger's sweetheart, and she signed Honoria. Dear me, that's not a common name, Honoria, is it? There's no lady in this house that signs Honoria, is there? O no, I don't think so! O no, I don't think so! And not in the same hand, perhaps? O no, I don't think so!'

'Honoria' – the dishonoured. It is a revelation, in a phase of the story full of revelations. But there are still things we do not know. Why did Hawdon and his Honoria not marry?

Should we sympathise with Sir Leicester *in extremis*?

In her revisionary (and influential) essay on *Bleak House*, Q. D. Leavis argued that, for all his preposterousness and snobbish self-regard, Sir Leicester is, at the end of the day, a gentleman;

more of a gentleman than Bucket, or even John Jarndyce. Dickens, in a master stroke, complicates our response to Sir Leicester's crowning humiliation by stressing that, whatever his absurdity, whatever his towering snobbishness, he truly loved Lady Dedlock. As the final paralysis approaches, more disabling than the gout or his own corseted observance of protocol, the baronet gazes into space:

> Heaven knows what he sees. The green, green woods of Chesney Wold, the noble house, the pictures of his forefathers, strangers defacing them, officers of police coarsely handling his most precious heir-looms, thousands of fingers pointing at him, thousands of faces sneering at him. But if such shadows flit before him to his bewilderment, there is one other shadow which he can name with something like distinctness even yet, and to which alone he addresses his tearing of his white hair and his extended arms.
>
> It is she, in association with whom, saving that she has been for years a main fibre of the root of his dignity and pride, he has never had a selfish thought. It is she whom he has loved, admired, honoured, and set up for the world to respect. It is she, who, at the core of all the constrained formalities and conventionalities of his life, has been a stock of living tenderness and love, susceptible as nothing else is of being struck with the agony he feels. He sees her, almost to the exclusion of himself; and cannot bear to look upon her cast down from the high place she has graced so well.

He then falls, stricken and capable only of mumbling, as he succumbs to the apoplexy that will paralyse him. His note to Bucket the next day: 'full forgiveness', is one of the more gracious gestures in the novel.

As the narrative progresses from this point and as Sir Leicester is increasingly broken down, he will becomes ever more dignified. As Mrs Rouncewell observes, the house of

Dedlock has finally succumbed to its ancient curse, but while the house of Dedlock crumbles around him, our estimation of Sir Leicester rises, reversing the harsh Dickensian satire which earlier played over the baronet. See, for example, the commentary in Chapter 58, after his defence of Lady Dedlock to the absurdly snobbish Volumnia, and his insistence that 'I am on unaltered terms with Lady Dedlock':

> His formal array of words might have at any other time, as it has often had, something ludicrous in it, but at this time it is serious and affecting. His noble earnestness, his fidelity, his gallant shielding of her, his generous conquest of his own wrong and his own pride for her sake, are simply honourable, manly, and true. Nothing less worthy can be seen through the lustre of such qualities in the commonest mechanic, nothing less worthy can be seen in the best-born gentleman. In such a light both aspire alike, both rise alike, both children of the dust shine equally.

What, one may ask, has brought about this change of attitude in Dickens? Or was it there from the start, when Sir Leicester was first conceived and introduced, almost two years ago?

*

Instalment 18 (Chapters 57–59), August 1853

Summary

Esther is woken at the Jarndyce's London house, to accompany Bucket in the 'pursuit'. The aim is not to capture Lady Dedlock, but to save her. Bucket on this occasion behaves with great gentleness. Building on the evidence of the handkerchief he has taken from Lady Dedlock's boudoir, he eventually deduces that she has gone to St Albans, some twenty-four miles away, on foot. Indeed she has, as we later learn, in order to take one last look at the daughter whom she believes to be at Bleak House.

Dickens accelerates the last section of the novel around 'the chase'. Their first call is to establish whether or not she has drowned herself, as do other 'unfortunates', in the Thames. They then take off for St Albans, by hired fast coach (in 1853 the journey could be accomplished in under an hour by train, but in the novel it takes the best part of the day to get there and back). On the way, Bucket enlightens Esther as to what really happened with Jo (whom the policeman calls 'Toughey'). To keep the boy from blabbing – particularly at Bleak House – Bucket bribed Skimpole with the usual fiver, at which the 'elderly young gentleman' (as Bucket describes him) betrayed the young street urchin, who was, as he earlier told Woodcourt, moved on. Bucket's devastating verdict on Skimpole is: 'No idea of money ... He takes it though!' This is the turning point in Esther's estimation of Skimpole (and, eventually, even John Jarndyce's).

211

In St Albans they call at the brickmaker's cottage. Lady Dedlock has been there and given the brutish father of the family her watch in exchange for Jenny's old clothes. Jenny has agreed to lay a false trail, wearing Lady Dedlock's clothes. It is snowing and Lady Dedlock, having failed in her intention to catch a last glimpse of Esther, is returning by foot to London (a round trip of some fifty miles). In London, Sir Leicester has made a partial recovery from his stroke and has indicated his intention to forgive his wife. He takes comfort in the return of George (who will, in fact, become his 'man', in succession to his mother).

When Bucket and Esther make their way, post haste, back to London, they meet up with Woodcourt, who has just been to call on Richard (and possibly Ada, who is newly pregnant). They learn that Lady Dedlock has left a letter at Snagsby's, but Guster, suffering a positive welter of fits, cannot produce the letter immediately. In the interim, Bucket convinces the comically suspicious Mrs Snagsby that her husband is not the illicit father of every waif and stray in London. When the letter is finally produced, it explains that Lady Dedlock went down to St Albans 'to see the dear one, if I could, once more – but only to see her – not to speak to her' and then, apparently, to end it all ('I must soon die' – how, she does not say). Guster reports, in her usual fitful way, that the lady has made her way to the squalid 'berryin ground' where Nemo and Jo have been laid to rest. They follow and at the gate of the cemetery see a prostrate figure. Esther, who has not understood the business with the swapped clothing assumes that it is Jenny. Bucket and Woodcourt let her go forward ('Her hands should be the first to touch her. They have a higher right than ours'). The corpse is, of course, 'my mother, cold and dead'. A tremendous finale.

*

The Thames: the poor person's graveyard

A favourite Victorian poem was Thomas Hood's 'Bridge of Sighs', published seven years before *Bleak House*. It sentimentally describes an 'unfortunate', who has drowned herself in the Thames:

> One more Unfortunate,
>   Weary of breath,
> Rashly importunate,
>   Gone to her death!
>
> Take her up tenderly,
>   Lift her with care;
> Fashion'd so slenderly
>   Young, and so fair!
>
> Look at her garments
>   Clinging like cerements;
> Whilst the wave constantly
>   Drips from her clothing;
>
> Take her up instantly,
>   Loving, not loathing.
> Touch her not scornfully;
> Think of her mournfully,
>   Gently and humanly;
> Not of the stains of her,
>
> All that remains of her
>   Now is pure womanly.
> Make no deep scrutiny
> Into her mutiny
>   Rash and undutiful:
> Past all dishonour,
> Death has left on her
>   Only the beautiful.

Bucket's first call is to the police booth by the Thames, and its morbid nightly list of those 'found drowned' – a favourite mode of suicide, particularly for women. An illustration, of Whistleresque gloom, was commissioned from Browne, showing Bucket and Esther on the bridge. Dickens worked up this theme later in the opening of *Our Mutual Friend*. The subject evidently fascinated him.

Strange, very strange

When Esther and Bucket call at the brickmaker's hovel (on the track of Lady Dedlock) the brickmaker (whose name we never know, nor care to find out) asks sharply who told them the lady had been there:

> 'A person of the name of Michael Jackson, with a blue welveteen waistcoat with a double row of mother of pearl buttons,' Mr. Bucket immediately answered.

The man gets everywhere.

Dickens and the feminist question: again

After visiting the brickmaker's cottage and witnessing the cowed and brutalised condition of the women of the household, Bucket observes:

> 'If time could be spared,' said Mr. Bucket, 'which is the only thing that can't be spared in this case, I might get it out of that woman; but it's too doubtful a chance to trust to under present circumstances. They are up to keeping a close eye upon her, and any fool knows that a poor creetur like her, beaten and kicked and scarred and bruised from head to foot, will stand by the husband that ill uses her through thick and thin.'

Bucket clearly understands domestic violence, but the law, as it stands in mid-Victorian England, is powerless to prevent it. Dickens, as clearly, feels a surge of protest. Nonetheless, it does not lessen his satire against Mrs Jellyby who, after the Borioboola-Gha scheme has gone bust:

> She has been disappointed in Borrioboola-Gha, which turned out a failure in consequence of the king of Boorioboola wanting to sell everybody – who survived the climate – for rum, but she has taken up with the rights of women to sit in Parliament.

If so, with John Stuart Mill at the head of the movement, Mrs Jellyby is one of the more historically significant characters in *Bleak House*.

How does Lady Dedlock die?

For the purpose of melodrama, Lady Dedlock dies very conveniently: at the gates of the burial ground where her former lover rests – just at the moment that her daughter, Bucket, and Woodcourt arrive. But what, precisely, should be on her death certificate? Some critics argue that she has expired from an infection of smallpox picked up from her earlier contact with Jo, but that was many months in the past, longer than the usual incubation period of the disease. Other critics suggest exhaustion, but travelling (largely on foot, we gather), the twenty-odd miles between the West End and St Albans should not be too great an ordeal for a well-fed, strong woman in her mid-forties. What seems most probable (and what Bucket and Woodcourt seem to have guessed), is that like Nemo/Hawdon, she has ended it all with opium, or some other poison that she took from her boudoir when she left Sir Leicester's town house. As she writes in her last letter: 'Cold, wet, and fatigue are sufficient causes for my being found dead; but I shall die of others'.

*

Instalments 19 & 20 (Chapters 60–67),

September 1853

Summary

After the awful discovery of her dead mother at the gates of the cemetery where her father is buried, Esther falls ill. She is nursed back to health in London. Allan Woodcourt and (by invitation of John Jarndyce) Allan's mother, are in constant attendance. The reason for this visit, engineered by Esther's guardian, we shall soon discover. John Jarndyce has used his influence to acquire for Allan a post as a medical attendant to the poor in Yorkshire.

Miss Flite, ominously, tells Esther that she has added two more birds to her aviary of Chancery hell: Richard and Ada. Vholes (whom Esther now sees as a 'Vampire'), confides that he disapproves of 'Mr C's marriage' – presumably on the grounds that it wastes his, Mr Vholes's, money. Ada is now pregnant. Esther makes a last, forlorn, attempt to persuade Skimpole to desist from conspiring to impoverish Richard, but the dilettante is as slippery as ever, although Esther does confront him with the evidence of his betrayal of Jo. When John Jarndyce learns of this, even he can no longer sustain his regard for Skimpole. The connection is severed, and with it, the flow of largesse to Skimpole. Five years later, we are told, Skimpole dies leaving a diary which contains, among other self-serving slander, 'Jarndyce, in common with most other men I have known, is the Incarnation of Selfishness.'

Allan Woodcourt declares his love to Esther and proposes

217

marriage. Although she has never openly discussed her engagement to John Jarndyce, after her acceptance of his offer, Esther regards herself as spoken for. She truly loves Allan, but is obliged to decline. Nonetheless, she is uplifted by his proposal: 'he had called me the beloved of his life'. John Jarndyce, who has been watching attentively, asks – in their code of love – when they will 'give Bleak House its mistress'. In a month's time, she says.

Bucket brings Old Smallweed to the house. The old skinflint has discovered, among Krook's rubble, a will which clearly disposes of the Jarndyce fortune – the bulk of it to Richard and Ada. By judicious bludgeoning, Bucket gets Smallweed to hand it over.

George sells up his shooting gallery and enters the service of the disabled Sir Leicester Dedlock. But first he takes a trip to the iron country to see his brother. Rosa, he discovers, is being sent to Germany with one of the Ironmaster's daughters, to be 'finished'. For reasons that are not immediately apparent, George wishes his brother to persuade his mother to remove him from her will. He also tells his brother (who is somewhat appalled) that he intends to enter Sir Leicester's 'Household Brigade' – he is going into service, like his mother. George has written a letter to Esther, explaining the circumstances of her father, Captain Hawdon's death. He was reported drowned and never resurfaced to deny the fact, preferring, for his own reasons, to become unknown.

John Jarndyce gives Esther £200 for 'their' wedding, with many coy references to her becoming mistress of Bleak House. Eventually, his ruse is revealed. They go to Yorkshire where he shows her another 'Bleak House', for her and Woodcourt to live in. He has divined that she really loves the other man, and has decided that he will not stand in the lovers' way. Indeed, he will make that way easier for them. The indomitable Guppy, meanwhile, comes to renew his suit and is promptly dismissed.

Kenge, with the new evidence of the will, re-enters the picture. It seems the great case of Jarndyce versus Jarndyce will at last be settled. When it is brought to final judgement, the putative beneficiaries discover that the whole vast treasure originally in dispute, has been eaten up by the costs of the court case. Richard has a physical collapse and dies. Sir Leicester survives, a shell of his former self, attended by George with the still absurd Volumnia as his housekeeper.

The last chapter is a retrospect, seven years on, from Esther Woodcourt, as she now is, the mother of two daughters and the fond godmother of Ada's son. Caddy too is a mother, whose child is deaf and dumb (Dickens had become interested in such children, and how they could be helped, in his visit to America in the early 1840s).

*

Vholes = Dracula?

Vholes, as Esther notes, has become thinner, blacker and more cadaverous the more he has feasted on Richard. 'So bloodless and gaunt,' she says, 'I felt as if Richard were wasting away beneath the eyes of this adviser, and there was something of the Vampire in him'. Dickens, of course, is thinking of the 'penny blood', *Varney the Vampire* by Thomas P. Prest, but it is pleasant to fancy that young Bram Stoker might have read this section of the novel, and lodged the detail, seed-like, in his brain. The story of the lawyer's clerk, Johnathan Harker, the legal deeds he brings with him to Castle Dracula and the fate

Plate 33. Attorney and Client, Fortitude and Impatience
– Vholes advises Richard

that befalls him and Lucy curiously redolent of the Richard–
Ada–Vholes triangle.

Dickens: north and south

The contrast between the industrial north and the old rural
south of England obsessed novelists in the 1850s. Mrs Gaskell
actually wrote a novel at this period entitled *North and South*
in which the heroine bounces like a pinball between the two
regions – as different for the Victorians as two continents.
Dickens, the most Cockney of novelists, would write his only
novel set outside London, *Hard Times*, immediately after *Bleak
House*. It grows, quite clearly, out of George Rouncewell's trip
in Chapter 63, to the Iron Country of the north where his
brother has made his fortune. Dickens's descriptions of the
north (here and in *Hard Times*), are like something out of
Piranesi:

> He comes to a gateway in the brick wall, looks in, and sees a great perplexity of iron lying about in every stage and in a vast variety of shapes – in bars, in wedges, in sheets; in tanks, in boilers, in axles, in wheels, in cogs, in cranks, in rails; twisted and wrenched into eccentric and perverse forms as separate parts of machinery; mountains of it broken up, and rusty in its age; distant furnaces of it glowing and bubbling in its youth; bright fireworks of it showering about under the blows of the steam-hammer; red-hot iron, white-hot iron, cold-black iron; an iron taste, an iron smell, and a Babel of iron sounds.

What one feels here is Victorian awe at their own gargantuan achievements. The north was not merely powerful in its factories; its schooling and development of education for the masses was in advance of the efforts of the south. As Esther discovers when she is recovering from the smallpox in Chesney Wold, the villagers of the 'pretty village' are largely illiterate. Rosa, the village beauty, would presumably be no dab hand at lettering if she had been left where fate first deposited her. In the north, however, with the Ironmaster's family, she is educated and sent off to Germany to cultivate herself in preparation for her marriage to Watt.

Hawdon's death: the last piece of the jigsaw

George writes a letter to Esther, while clearing up other details in his life, explaining the exact circumstances in which Captain Hawdon died. They are revealing:

> He was (officially) reported drowned, and assuredly went over the side of a transport-ship at night in an Irish harbour within a few hours of her arrival from the West Indies, as I have myself heard both from officers and men on board, and know to have been (officially) confirmed.

His financial circumstances evidently made it advisable that he stay officially drowned, rather than face court martial. But we still do not know (and never will), why he deserted his pregnant Honoria (while keeping her letters). Where did she become pregnant? Surely not in the West Indies. Did he abandon her after, or before, Esther was born? Before, perhaps, he knew that Honoria was with child.

Did Dickens believe in the afterlife?

Probably, like most of his readers, Dickens did believe in the afterlife. This makes the necessarily pathetic climax to Richard's death. He dies, more handsome than Esther has ever seen him, repeating that – now the case is settled – he will 'begin the world' – start over. His last words are to his wife (attended by Allan and Esther):

> He sought to raise himself a little. Allan raised him so that she could hold him on her bosom; which was what he wanted.
> 'I have done you many wrongs, my own. I have fallen like a poor stray shadow on your way, I have married you to poverty and trouble, I have scattered your means to the winds. You will forgive me all this, my Ada, before I begin the world?'
> A smile irradiated his face, as she bent to kiss him. He slowly laid his face down upon her bosom, drew his arms closer round her neck, and with one parting sob began the world. Not this world, O not this! The world that sets this right.
> When all was still, at a late hour, poor crazed Miss Flite came weeping to me, and told me she had given her birds their liberty.

The Victorian reader's eyes would moisten, without embarrassment, at this religiosity. Not, perhaps, those of the modern viewer.

Plate 34. Light

The Esther problem: unresolved to the end

Modern readers may well have difficulty with Esther's last words in the novel, which seem self-satisfied and perhaps, dare one say it, somewhat Skimpolish:

> The people even praise me as the doctor's wife. The people even like me as I go about, and make so much of me that I am quite abashed. I owe it all to him, my love, my pride! They like me for his sake, as I do everything I do in life for his sake.

> Can Esther, bathed as she is in the admiration of everyone who comes across her, from Brickmaker's slatternly wife to Inspector Bucket (that professional misanthrope), really be so naive?

*

Afterword

Novels, as the term indicates, are intrinsically 'new' things. What does *Bleak House* – a novel a century-and-a-half old – have to say to us?

The social issues in this mid-Victorian novel are (alas) still with us: from traffic congestion; through the bureaucratic ineptitude of the law (still an ass, still unconscionably slow, still damnably expensive); drug addiction; the plight of the socially-excluded underclass; pollution; poverty (still not 'made history'). Dickens still shines a light on the dark places of our society.

Bleak House is also one of the great human comedies in our literature. Even in the most heart-rending numbers there is laugh-out-loud, characteristically *Dickensian* humour, reflecting a rare ability to mix the comic, pathetic, and socially relevant. The instruction 'Enjoy!' could be posted at the head of every instalment of *Bleak House* – and one still does enjoy.

Above all, to read and watch *Bleak House* is to gain a sense of what it was to be Victorian, and in turn, to better understand ourselves. Victorian Britain is the foundation on which our age rests, not least in the standards of duty and decency which guide us (as they guide Esther, Allan, and John Jarndyce), through our lives.

The BBC's version of *Bleak House* will partner the novelist's genius with the dramatic genius of Andrew Davies, introducing millions of viewers to Dickens's masterpiece. They will be enriched by the experience.

As I say, 'Enjoy!'

J&J